A Book for Government Officials to Master *Noting* and *Drafting*

... on physical and e-files

M.K. Agarwal

Revised and Enlarged by

Professor Shital Prakash

and

Dr. Bhawna Gupta

PUSTAK MAHAL®

Publishers
Pustak Mahal®

Administrative office and sale centre

J-3/16 , Daryaganj, New Delhi-110002
☎ 011-23276539, 23272783, 23272784, 23260518
E-mail: info@pustakmahal.com
Website: www.pustakmahal.com

Branch
Bengaluru: ☎ 080-22234025, 40912845
E-mail: pustakmahalblr@gmail.com

ISBN 978-81-223-0984-3

Edition: 2026

Printed at: Radha Offset, Delhi

CONTENTS

FOREWORD

Good governance has been recognized as the primary reason behind the most remarkable success stories of developed countries who are enjoying great prosperity and are able to provide socio-economic welfare to their citizens. It is widely perceived that India's poor record in economic and social front is largely due to poor governance. It is therefore, imperative that we put in place a governance model that is citizens friendly and provides efficient, cost effective services to them. This calls for developing strong, vibrant and dynamic public organizations which are sensitive to people's needs. This is possible only if the personnel working there embrace change and modernize the organizations, keeping pace with rapid development in information technology, space and avionics which has crushed time and space.

The Senior Citizens' Council for Human Resource Development is an autonomous institution of the Public Management Development Foundation, a registered public charitable trust. The Council has been established for involving in dignified manner, intellectuals and professionals having rich experience, technical qualifications and skills sets in various disciplines with a view to work towards creation of efficient and dynamic public organizations by educating and training the personnel working there and doing research in frontier areas of public administration and publish those studies. The Council has developed a new philosophy of public administration to meet the, '21st Century Challenges to Public Management', so that public managers could effectively deal with the complex problems confronting them and fulfill the aspirations of people whom they are expected to serve. The book on, 'A book for Government Official to Master Noting and Drafting', is in furtherance of the objectives of the Senior Citizens' Council for Human Resource Development and is intended as training material for personnel working at grass root level in public institutions, so that they become efficient on their job and contribute to organizational productivity.

The personnel working in public organizations are responsible for the decisions they take and are accountable for their actions while implementing those decisions. These obligations are discharged by way of notings on the files, which show the circumstances and the considerations which weighed in making those decisions. For conveying the decisions accurately and clearly good drafting is essential. Therefore, both noting and drafting are basic ingredients of good administration. Realizing the importance of noting and drafting, the Senior Citizens' Council for Human Resource Development has been conducting training programmes for personnel working in government organizations, under the stewardship of Shri M.K. Agarwal and Professor Shital Parkash. The Council also requested Shri Agarwal to write a book which can inform, instruct and guide the staff and officers working in public institutions, the salient features of good noting and drafting. Shri Agarwal has more than fulfilled the expectation of the Council and has come out with an excellent training and educational guide. Realizing the needs of a learner, Shri Agarwal has put the material in simple, lucid and reader friendly manner. An added feature of the book is large number of exercises with their solutions at the end of each chapter, which can help a learner in reinforcing the ideas presented in the book.

Shri M.K. Agarwal has excellent credentials to write a book on noting and drafting. He was Senior Faculty Member of the Institute of Secretariat Training and Management of the Government of India and has authored a book, "Administrative Work Study", besides several academic papers on administrative reforms. He has 36 years of experience of working in the Government of India in senior positions and retired as Deputy Secretary in the Ministry of Home Affairs.

With the passing of Right to Information Act, the Parliament has given the people of this country full access to information on matters relating to governance. Noting on the file are crucial to access to information as they give the background against which decisions are taken. An eminent commentator observes, 'Notes are the live-wires in the decision making process. Snap them and you are plunged in darkness'. In the context of making the working of government transparent and accountable, the personnel working in government should understand the importance of noting and strive to improve on their writing style and content.

I congratulate Shri M.K. Agarwal for producing a scholarly book of great practical utility to persons working in government and allied institutions. I also compliment Professor Shital Parkash, Managing Director of the Council for encouraging the writing of the book and making untiring efforts to see that the book is published.

The book fulfills an important need of personnel working in public institutions and I commend its use by them.

B.P. Mathur, IA and AS (Retd.)
Ph.D., D. Litt.
President Senior Citizens' Council
for Human Resource Development
(Formerly Deputy Comptroller and Auditor General of India,
Chairman, Audit Board of India and
Director National Institute of Financial Management)

PREFACE

Noting and drafting are two important activities in Government organizations. Noting show *how* and *why* a particular decision was made and *what* had been the contribution of the functionaries in the decision-making chain; drafting shows the skill of these functionaries in tactfully conveying the decision.

Basic note on a file is usually written by an Assistant, who also does the drafting (although in some offices, the clerical staff – lower division clerks and upper division clerks – also do this work). While writing the note, the functionary concerned is expected to define the issue under consideration; analyze it; point out the provisions of Acts, Rules, Regulations, policy, and precedents, if any, that have a bearing on the case; bring out clearly the point or points requiring a decision; discuss alternative ways in which the issue can be tackled and the consequences of each such way; suggest the best way in which it should be tackled, and explain why that is the most appropriate way. The decision finally reached is to be conveyed to the party concerned. For this purpose, a draft is prepared. A good draft is expected to be complete, clear, concise, correct, coherent, and courteous.

It has been noticed that in many organizations, the staff does not have a clear idea of what is expected in a note; nor are they familiar with the various forms of communication and the way they are written. Therefore, they do not provide much support to their officers in these activities. This reality came in focus when the Senior Citizens' Council for Human Resource Development recently conducted a series of training programmes on Noting and Drafting for the staff of some Government organizations. It was found that the contribution of the staff was limited to putting up receipts in files, summarizing or paraphrasing the receipts, and submitting them to their officers for orders. In most cases, officers themselves have to prepare drafts. It was also found that there were no institutional arrangements for regularly training the staff and developing their skills in noting and drafting. Unlike earlier times when there was adequate time with everyone to give attention to such matters, in the fast pace of the present-day work, supervisory officers have little time – and patience – to train and guide their staff in these skills. The Council, then, realized the need to fill this gap, and took up the project of preparing a book on the subject. Hence this book.

Notes and drafts are forms of written communication. Notes are internal communications that provide a link between the reasoning and the decision within the organization. Drafts, after these are polished and finalized, become external communications that provide a link between the organization and the outside agencies. Both are, therefore, crucial for efficient and effective functioning of the organization.

Notes and drafts are pieces of writing. Their effectiveness depends on the writing skills of the writer. Effective writing means that the writer answers all possible questions that may arise while considering a problem; expresses himself in a language that is easily understood and is free from confusion or ambiguity; and presents it attractively. Such writing is likely to generate feelings of confidence and trust, and get a favourable response from the reader. It will also help in reducing the cost of processing of cases because backtracking would be avoided, and their prompt disposal would be ensured.

This book is an attempt to help, instruct, and guide the functionaries in offices to develop their writing skills, make them aware of what is expected of them when processing cases, enable them to improve the quality of their notes and drafts, and make meaningful contribution in the disposal of work.

The unique features of this book are that it elucidates the essentials of effective writing, explains the salient features of processing and analysis of cases and of noting and drafting, discusses the key points of the main forms of written communications that are used in Government organizations, and reinforces the learning through a number of exercises at the end of each chapter.

Chapter 1 lays the foundations for developing effective writing skill. It discusses the principles of effective writing; guides the reader how to put these principles in practice; and tells how the written piece should be organized and presented.

Chapter 2 explains the general principles of processing of cases; discusses the various steps involved in opening of files; and guides the reader about the procedure for bringing receipts on files, examining them, and putting them up.

Chapter 3 tells about the main forms of written communications used in offices; highlights the key features of each one of them; and shows the format of these communications.

Chapter 4 describes the essential features of notes; guides the reader about what to write in notes; informs of the guidelines for preparing notes; tells about the action to be taken when it is proposed to modify notes or orders; and points out the steps to be taken when writing notes on the files of other organizations or under the single file system.

Chapter 5 tells about what is a draft; what is the procedure for preparing drafts; and explains the instructions that should be followed when corresponding with State

Governments or their Ministers, Members of Parliament, constitutional or statutory authorities, and members of the public.

Each of these chapters is followed by a number of exercises designed to reinforce the points made in the text of the chapter. The progress in learning the key points can be tested through solving these exercises and checking the answers with those given after the exercises.

Whatever has been written in this book is based on my long experience in Government service, the study of the relevant literature, and the experience gained during inter-action with participants of the training programmes. All this has been so internalized that it is not possible to name any single person to whom I can express my gratitude. Nevertheless, I am sincerely thankful to all of them for the ideas that came from them, and many of which have been included in the book.

I am grateful to the Senior Citizen's Council for Human Resource Development for giving me an opportunity for sharing my knowledge and understanding of the concepts of writing notes and drafts with a wider audience.

I am also grateful to the Council's President, Dr. B. P. Mathur, M.A., Ph.D., D.Litt, I.A. and A.S. (Retd.), formerly Deputy Comptroller and Auditor General of India, Chairman of Audit Board of India and Director National Institute of Financial Management for his dynamic leadership and encouragement throughout the duration of this project.

I am deeply indebted to Professor Shital Parkash, Managing Director of the Council and a long-time friend and colleague, for inspiring me to take up this project, and providing invaluable help and guidance at its every stage. His unstinted support was crucial for successful completion of this project.

I express my gratitude to another long-time friend and colleague, Mr. Dev Raj Sharma for his valuable suggestions in preparing this book.

I am thankful to Ms. Renu Jaswal who painstakingly and ungrudgingly worked on the manuscript and gave it a presentable shape.

In the end, I express my sincere thanks to our publishers M/s Pustak Mahal, who so graciously accepted the book for publication and brought it out in record time.

M. K. AGARWAL

PREFACE TO TWO THOUSAND TWENTY-TWO EDITION

Office operations comprise such activities as establishment, store purchase and store–accounting, house-keeping and of course, receipt and dispatch of communications, handling of files, processing of cases through noting and drafting. These and other backroom operations are performed by office staff to facilitate their officers.

'Paperless office' deemed to be only a utopia few decades ago. Now, however, electronic technology and software development are transforming traditional offices into virtual offices. Now one can do any office work anytime from anywhere provided there is strong internet network, a desktop/laptop or a tablet or even a smart mobile telephone. Online operations are replacing manual operations. Banking system is totally digitized. Tele-medicine is replacing physical OPDs. Courts have started working through video-conferencing. Many organisations are operating only online. India is the first country to have introduced EVM in elections at all the three levels- Lok Sabha, Vidhan Sabha and Urban Local Bodies and Panchayats.

Initially tracking of papers and files was taken up electronically. Now, however, receipt, registration, distribution of dak, processing of cases through noting and drafting, outward communication and retrieval have been started being performed electronically. Earlier than later, there will be no physical file, only e-files. All old records are being digitized. National Informatics Centre (NIC) and some other organisations have developed comprehensive software packages and governments after governments are changing over to e-offices.

Few years back, Senior Citizens' Council for Human Resource Development had brought out books in English, Hindi and bilingually in English and Hindi on noting and drafting under the authorship of the revered Late. Mr. M.K. Agrawal. There has been great response to these books and these are in great demand even today. In these books, Mr. Agrawal talked about noting and drafting in the context of physical files. Unfortunately, he is no longer with us to update these books. We have been well advised to update these books and include there in noting and drafting on e-files. We also had similar feedback from many of the participants who had attended large number of training programmes we organised on the subject for many organisations.

We studied the latest 'Central Secretariat Manual of Office Procedures.' It has incorporated the working of e-office. We visited a number of organisations which have changed their traditional offices into e-offices. We saw officers working on e-files. We studied the system in detail and discussed the matter with officers working therein. We also had hands-on experience of the system. Thus, equipped with the knowledge and experience of e-files, we have thoroughly revised the earlier books and are happy to bring out these revised books on noting and drafting. The revision has kept the original base of physical files intact and has brought in generous intervention of e-files wherever required. This approach will enable the reader to understand and master the skill of noting and drafting both on physical and e-files. We are sure that readers will welcome the revised version as they have been happy with older editions. We pay our deepest regards to our old colleague and friend Late M.K. Agrawal, the original great author of these great books. We are amazed with his knowledge and experience of this field and how lucidly and clear headedly he had written these books. Hats off to him. We are grateful to his son, Dr. Arvind K. Agrawal, who graciously encouraged us to take up this revision.

We are grateful to Senior Citizens' Council for Human Resource Development for giving us this opportunity to revise these books on noting and drafting which have great demand in the market. We are thankful to Ms. Renu Jaswal who painstakingly and ungrudgingly worked on the manuscript and gave these a presentable shape. We also express our sincere thanks to M/S Pustak Mahal, who so graciously accepted the revised versions and brought these out in record time.

Shital Parkash

Bhawna Gupta

Chapter - One

COMMON TERMS USED IN OFFICE PROCESSING

1. **'Appendix to correspondence'** in relation to a file means lengthy enclosures to a communication (whether receipt or issue) on the file, inclusion of which in the correspondence portion is likely to obstruct smooth reading of the correspondence or make the correspondence portion unwieldy.

2. **'Appendix to notes'** in relation to a file means a lengthy summary or statement containing detailed information concerning certain aspects of the question discussed on the file, incorporation of which in the main note is likely to obscure the main point or make the main note unnecessarily lengthy. Such aspects are processed in Appendix to Notes and key issues arising therefrom are then processed in the Notes portion giving reference to the relevant page in Appendix to Notes.

3. **'Branch'**- The Unit of a Division and may comprise a couple of Sections/Units/Cells.

4. **'Branch Officer'** in relation to a section means the officer, Under Secretary, Deputy Director or equivalent, who is directly above the section in the line of control for execution of work.

5. **CAMS:** Collaboration and Messaging Service is a tightly integrated communication module providing secure internal information sharing to individuals/groups with features for initiating discussions using forums. It includes modules like-mail, calendar, photo gallery and eConnect services.

6. **'Case'** means a current file or a receipt together with other related papers, if any.

7. **'Central Issue Section'** means the unit within a Department responsible for dispatch of communication to the addresses and includes functionaries like resident clerk and night duty clerk.

8. **'Central Receipt and Issue Section'** means a unit within a Department consisting of the central registry and the central issue section.

9. **'Central Registration Unit (CRU)'** means a unit within a Department assigned with the responsibility of receiving, registering and distributing dak meant for that Department and includes functionaries like resident clerk and night duty clerk. Often, the terms Central Issue Section, Central Receipt and Issue Section and CRU are used inter-changeably.

10. **'Classified dak'** means dak bearing a security grading.

11. **'Chief Executive'** means Chairman/Chairman and Managing Director / Managing Director/ Director General / Director, of the organization concerned.

12. **'Come-back case'** means a case received back for further action such as reexamination or preparing a draft or a summary of the case.

13. **'Corporation/ Company/Board/Department or any other organization'** means the full name of the organization concerned including Corporate Office/ Headquarters, and other offices of the organization concerned.

14. **'Correspondence portion'** in relation to a file means the portion containing 'receipts' and office copies of 'issue' pertaining to the file including self-contained inter-departmental notes but excluding those recorded on the notes portion of the file itself.

15. **'C.R.U. No.'** means the serial number assigned by the Central Registration Unit to dak in the dak register.

16. **'Current file'** means a file action on which has not been completed.

17. **'Dak'** includes every type of written communication such as letter, telegram, fax, interdepartmental note, or file, which is received, whether by post or otherwise, in the organization concerned for its consideration.

18. **'Dealing hand'** means any functionary such as an Executive, an Assistant, or a Clerk, entrusted with initial examination and noting upon cases.

19. **'Diarising'** means registering of receipts in the Section Diary. 14. 'Diary number' means the serial number assigned to a receipt in the Section Diary followed by code letters identifying the Section Diary ('H' for section diary for Hindi receipts and 'O' for section diary for other receipts), the year and the abbreviated symbol of the section, e.g. 315-H/10-Estt.I. 15. 'Docketing' means making of entries in the notes portion of a file about the serial number assigned to each item of correspondence (whether receipt or issue) for its identification.

20. **'Diarist'** means a clerk within a Section charged with the responsibility, inter alia, of maintaining the Section Diary.

21. **DSC (Digital Signature Certificate) or Electronic Signature:** The Information Technology Act, 2000 and the subsequent Amendment Act 2008 provides for use of digital signatures (and now termed as electronic signatures) on the documents submitted in electronic form in order toensure the security and authenticity of the documents filed electronically. An electronic (digital) signature is the electronic equivalent of a handwritten signature, verifying the authenticity of electronic documents. These electronic signatures are stored in a certificate which stores the personal information of the owner which is then imported to a physical device (USB Token, floppy disk, CD etc.).

Dos:

a) The token containing certificate should be preserved in safe custody by the owner of the certificate.

b) If the token is lost, the concerned certifying authority (CA) should be informed and requested for the revocation of the certificate immediately.

c) The owner should always ensure to protect the private key with a good password.

Don'ts:

a) The private key protected by a password should never be sent across any network

b) Never delete token objects, as once, deleted objects will never be regained.

22. **e-file Administrator:**e-file Administrator is the identified person in any Department who holds privileged rights to manage all the reference data, transfer of cases, reports permissions, search privileges etc. in case of e-file.

23. **e-file:** File Management System or e-file, provides a simplified, accountable, responsive, effective and transparent electronic systemfor end-to-end processing of any file. The system includesall stages of working on a file, right from registration of an inward receipts to creation of file, to noting, drafting, approval, signing andissuingof a communication of decisions. With thissystem, the movement of receiptsand files becomes seamless with ease of access to endusers as every action taken on a receipt or file is recorded electronically. This automation of file plays a verycrucial role in both improving the efficiency of decision making and bringing transparency in government.

24. **e-Leave:** Leave Management System: An automatedworkflow based system for managing the complete life-cycle of a leave application from application of leave-requests to sanctioning of leaves., with subsequent joining requests. The system provides a robust admin interface for the product administrator to manage

leaves/approval workflow in an efficient manner with various Reports to facilitate seamless use.

25. **e-Office:** e-Office is a product suite aimed at transforming the core of the Government functioning, the work culture and work ethics by bringing in more efficiency, transparency, and accountability in Government transactions leading to increased productivity. One of the key areas of importance in e-Office is to have a uniform and seamless communication channel between the electronic world (User-Department Implementing e-Office) and the existing physical world (extremal organisations, citizen etc.). e-Office includes many different modules in it which are: e-file, KMS, e-Leave, e-Tour, PIS/eService book and CAMS.

26. **e-Office Administrator:**e-Office Administrator is the identified user with all the administrative privileges end rights to manage various master/reference data, and its configuration of all the available applications of e-Office product suites vize-file, e-Leave, e-Tour, PIMS and CAMS. He is the one with the responsibility of creation, mapping, and management of all the organization and user data of the e-Office.

27. **e-Tour:** Tour Management System-An automated workflow based system for approval of domestic/international tour to disbursement of advance for tour to its claim and settlement.

28. **'File'** means a collection of papers on a specific subject matter assigned a file number and consisting of one or more of the following parts: (a) Correspondence (b) Notes (c) Appendix to correspondence (d) Appendix to notes

29. **'Final disposal'** in relation to a case under consideration means completion of all action thereon culminating, where necessary, in the issue of final orders or final reply to the party from which the original communication emanated.

30. **'Fresh receipt (FR)'** means any subsequent receipt on a case which brings in additional information to aid the disposal of a paper under consideration.

31. **'Indexing'** in relation to a file means indicating its title under appropriate catchwords arranged in their alphabetical order with a view to facilitate its location in the event of need. 20. 'Index slip' means a card or a paper slip displaying the title of the file under a catchword followed by a reference to its file number. 21. 'Issue' means an outgoing communication issued in a case. 22. 'Director' means Director of the organization concerned.

32. **'Information and Facilitation Counter (IFC)'** is a facility, normally set-up outside the Security Zone of Ministries/Department/Organizationsto provide information to the citizens/clients about the programmes, schemes, etc. as well as status of cases, applications, etc. IFCs are also called 'May I Help You' or 'Help' Counters in certain organizations.

33. **IT Cell:** Each Department must have an IT Cell to administer and manage the e-Officedata-base as an e-Office and e-file administrator. Till the time such IT cell is created, the Department will designate an officer and a team to carry out these functions. Illustrative list of functions of IT Cell are:

   a. To create government mail IDs for the users who do not have one and also to map the existing IDs to their respective e-Office application.

   b. To manage the employee transfer and joining.

   c. To manage the DSCs provided to various employees

   d. To give training to the new users in working of e-Office

   e. To manage the master and reference data with respect to various applications of e-Office

34. **KMS:** Knowledge Management System- Government manages large volume of documents of various categories like Policies, Forms, Circulars, Guidelines, etc. Maintaining a central repository ofdocuments provides a one stop access of all the necessary information required by endusers in the Department. KMS allowusers to create and managee-documents which can be viewed, searched and shared. It is also capable of keeping track of the different versions modified by different users.

35. **Meta-data:** Meta-data are details of information provided in the pre-defined fields for a Dak while registration and/or for a file during its creation

36. **'Note'** means the remarks recorded on a case to facilitate its disposal.

37. **'Notes portion'** in relation to a file means the portion containing notes recorded on a case.

38. **'Paper under consideration (PUC)'** means a receipt on a case, the consideration of which is the subject matter of the case.

39. **'Personal staff'** in relation to a functionary means and includes private secretary, personal assistant, stenographer, assistant, clerk or any other clerical staff or personnel in the personal sections appointed to assist the Chief Executive and other senior executives of the organization concerned.

40. **'PIS'**: Personal Information System or e-ServiceBook.

41. **'Precedent Book'** is a register in a prescribed format to keep note of important rulings and decisions having a precedent value for ready reference.

42. **'Receipt'** means dak after it has been received by the concerned dealing hand.

43. **'Record Clerk'** means a clerk in a section responsible inter alia for typing and maintaining index slips and for looking after routine aspects of recording work.

'Record Clerk' in relation to Branch Record Room or Central Record Room means a clerk in the respective Record Room responsible for receiving, maintaining, and issuing recorded files.

44. **'Recording'** means the process of closing a file after action on all the issues considered thereon has been completed, and includes operations like completing references, removing routine papers, revising the file title, changing the file cover, and stitching the file. 30. 'Reference folder' in relation to a particular subject means a folder containing copies of relevant rules, orders, instructions, etc., arranged in chronological order.

45. '**Registration**' means entering of details of dak at the entry level.

46. '**Registration at entry level**' means that in e-file, a dak or an inward communication is registered only once at the first point of entry in a Department, whether in the CRU or in the personal offices of the Minister, Secretary or any other officer or in the Section.

47. '**Registration number**'means the serial number assigned to a dak by the e-file system after registration. It is also referred to as CRU number.

48. '**Registration Officer**' means a functionary within a section or in CRU or in the personal section of an officer entrusted with the responsibility of registration of dak, marking and sending of receipts and files and other associated tasks.

49. **'Routine note'** means a note of a temporary value or ephemeral importance recorded outside the file, e.g., a record of casual discussion or a note on a point of secondary importance intended to facilitate consideration of the case by higher officers.

50. **'Running summary of facts'** in relation to a case means a summary of the facts of the case updated from time to time to incorporate significant developments as and when they take place.

51. **'Section'** means the basic work unit, responsible for attending to items of work allotted to it. It is generally headed by a Section Officer.

52. **'Section officer'** means an officer supervising a Section.

53. **'Sectional note'** means a note recorded on only one of the many issues raised in the PUC.

54. **'Security grading'** means security marking 'Confidential', 'Secret', or 'Top Secret'.

55. **'Shadow file'** is a file maintained bya Section to which another Section sends its file for advice/ clarification, etc.

56. **'Standard Head'** means 'Functional Head' followed by a dash, then 'main head' followed by separator '0', and then 'sub-head'.

57. **'Standard process sheet'** means a standard skeleton note developed for a repetitive item of work, indicating predetermined points of check or aspects to be noted upon.

58. **'Standing guard file'** on a subject means a compilation consisting of the following three parts: (a) a running summary of the principles and policy relating to the subject with number and date of relevant decisions or orders quoted in margin against each; (b) copies of the decisions or orders referred to, arranged in chronological order; and (c) model forms of communications to be used at different stages.

59. **'Standing note'** in relation to a subject means a continuing note explaining, among other things, the history and development of the policy and procedure, designed to serve as: (a) a complete background material for review of the existing policy or procedure; (b) a brief for preparing replies to Questions in Parliament / State Legislatures or notes for supplementaries thereto; and (c) induction or training material.

60. **'Urgent dak'** means dak marked 'immediate' or 'priority', and includes telegrams, fax, wireless messages, telex messages, and e-mails.

***

Chapter - Two

WRITING EFFECTIVELY

1. INTRODUCTION

1.1 Writing is thought on paper. It is a tool that helps in creating and organizing ideas. When you put your random ideas on paper, you begin to understand them better. As you continue to process and develop a polished document, you refine your ideas and express them more effectively.

1.2 Effective presentation of ideas requires that you should write clearly and accurately, and in a language that your readers can understand. You should write in a way that is attractive to the reader; otherwise, he may ignore your writing and may even have a negative reaction.

1.3 Clear and accurate writing is needed also because, in offices, a large number of written communications are received, and sent out, every day. Confused, complex and inaccurate communications will create misunderstanding and extra effort will be required to interpret their meaning correctly. Even excellent ideas will get defeated if the communication is poorly written and badly organized.

1.4 Besides, within offices, officers and employees spend a lot of time in reading the written word in the form of notes, instructions, reports, proposals and the like. They also spend time in writing notes and other forms of communications. They need clear, concise, complete, and correct writing. Nobody wants to wade through poorly written material. On the other hand, everyone looks forward to communications which convey information clearly, accurately and efficiently, so that quick and sound decisions may be made and instructions may be correctly followed. Therefore, there is a need for good writing in offices.

1.5 Good writing is a prized skill. It reflects your ability to think well – to analyse information, weigh alternatives, and make recommendations or decisions. If you have written well, you can enhance the organization's image, motivate people, and create good-will. Your writing will stand out from a mass of material that competes for attention in offices. You will, most likely, get a favourable response from your reader.

1.6 Herein we shall discuss how you can write lucidly and effectively, and present your writing attractively. The discussion is divided into the following five sections:

* write the way you talk
* streamline your writing: check for completeness, clarity, conciseness, coherence, correctness and courtesy
* organize your writing
* present your writing
* meet the deadline.

Writing is a skill. As with all skills, you can improve it through practice. This chapter will give you guidance about good writing, and, with practice, you can sharpen your skill.

2. WRITE THE WAY YOU TALK

2.1 The key to simple and clear writing is "to talk" on paper to your reader. When you are writing, imagine that you're actually standing in front of your reader, and then write those words that you would use in your "talk." If you do so, the words will come out like the best of speaking.

To "talk" on paper, you may have to change your writing style. For example, you may have to give up writing in which you:

* use less familiar words like <u>commence</u> instead of begin, or <u>prior</u> instead of before
* avoid punctuation marks except full stop and comma
* avoid using personal pronouns like "I", "we", and "you"

For simple and clear writing, you should:

* use simple, short, familiar words
* use a variety of punctuation
* use more personal pronouns
* use contractions (sometimes)

Let us examine these suggestions.

2.2 Use Simple, Short, Familiar Words

We take more time to read and understand a long and less familiar word (like facilitate) than a short and familiar word (like help). This difference may be small in time, but it strains our memory. This strain will be greatly reduced if we use simple, short, and familiar words like we use in spoken language. The document will also be beautiful in its simplicity and efficiency.

Here is a short list of some long, less familiar words and phrases, and their simpler equivalent:

Less familiar	Simpler equivalent
Aforementioned	These
By means of	By
Compensate	Pay
Consequently	So
Inasmuch as	Because
Indicate	Show, Tell
In the event that	If
In the near future	Soon
Terminate	End
Utilize	Use

Which of these words you use in your writing? The chances are that you would be using the words from the left-hand side, because these seem to be more "impressive". But by doing so, you would be making the reader's job harder. Simpler words on the right-hand side are easier to understand and are more precise.

Sometimes you may need some less familiar words as, for example, vocabulary for your profession. But in such cases, use them sparingly.

2.3 Use A Variety of Punctuation

Writing without the use of punctuation is like a speaker talking in monotone. No audience likes a speaker who talks to them in monotone, because it forces the audience to try to find out what was important in that sentence and what is going to be said in the next. Good speakers use hand gestures and voice inflection to help their listeners along. Punctuation marks in writing replace those hand gestures and voice inflection. With punctuation marks, the writing becomes more interesting, the writer brings variety, sentences become better, and emphasis and ideas are at the right place.

For example, look at this paragraph:

> According to our findings, the delay in the completion of the project was not due to the contractor, as we first suspected, but due to the government agencies which did not supply the materials to the contractor on time.

Now, see the difference after it is written with punctuation marks:

> Who was responsible for the delay in the completion of the project? Was it the contractor, as we had first suspected? Not at all: it were the <u>government agencies</u> which <u>did not supply</u> the materials on time.

You will notice that question marks, colon, and underlining have made it more interesting.

We are all familiar with punctuation marks, and quite often use full stops and commas in our writing. But some other punctuation marks, such as colon, semi-colon, dash, question mark, and apostrophe should also be used to make your writing interesting and easier to read.

2.4 Use More Pronouns

People often use personal pronouns in their conversation. In fact, you will be very uncomfortable if you do not use pronouns when you talk to people. But in office writing these pronouns are not used so that the writing is kept formal and objective. This is an outdated notion. In today's good writing, a more personal and informal tone is gaining wide acceptance.

Important personal pronouns are:

> **<u>First Person</u>:** I, me, my, mine, we, us, our, ours
> **<u>Second Person:</u>** you, your, yours

By using pronouns, it is likely that you use active—instead of passive—voice and your sentences will be easier to read. You can write more easily and accurately with pronouns.

There may be occasions when personal pronouns may not be required in your writing as, for example, that describes a machine or an equipment. But if you are writing about how to operate the machine or equipment, personal pronouns may have to be used.

The point is not that personal pronouns should always be used, but that don't try to avoid them.

2.5 Use Contractions (Sometimes)

Contractions do not improve readability. You may use them or write without them, and the writing will not become harder. But contractions do give an informal tone to your writing. It will not be correct if your writing always uses contractions. Same will be the case if you always write without using contractions. If you want to be closer to your reader, use contractions. But if you want to be formal and maintain an objective distance, the writing may be without contractions.

3. STREAMLINE YOUR WRITING: CHECK FOR COMPLETENESS, CLARITY, CONCISENESS, COHERENCE, CORRECTNESS, AND COURTESY

3.1 People differ in their attitudes, abilities, skills, and the meanings they attach to the words in use. They may not understand your writing in the same manner as you may have intended. Therefore, keep your readers in view and try to understand different interpretations that they may put to the words and sentences you choose. Streamline your writing to make it complete, clear, concise, coherent, correct, and courteous, so that favourable attitudes and opinions are formed and positive emotions are aroused.

3.2 Completeness

Your message will be complete when it contains all the facts your reader needs for the response you desire. A complete message saves expenses for additional messages for clarifications, and builds goodwill.

When you strive for completeness, you should:

* answer all questions asked
* give something extra, where necessary
* check for five Ws and other essentials

3.2.1 Answer All Questions Asked: Whenever you write a note, or draft a communication or a report, or reply to an enquiry, try to answer all questions—stated and unstated. The response to an incomplete document may be unfavourable; it may give rise to suspicion that either you are careless or you are trying to conceal something. Therefore, your note or draft should answer all possible questions of the matter under consideration. Even if you have unfavourable information to furnish, you should prepare your reply with tact and honesty.

Sometimes before you answer an enquiry, you may need specific information from the enquirer. In that case, list the needed details on a reply form that the enquirer can fill and return to you.

3.2.2 Give Something Extra, Where Necessary While writing a note or preparing a draft, you should give any additional information available in office, if such information may help in better understanding the question under consideration and making sound decisions.

Similarly, you must give more information even if the enquirers have not asked for it. They may not be clear what they need or their questions may be inadequate. For example, suppose you receive an enquiry about the availability of post-graduate courses in your institution. If you list only the names of the courses available, the reply will be incomplete. You should also give information about eligibility conditions and recognition accorded to those courses, so that the enquirer may decide right away about joining a course.

3.2.3 Check For Five Ws And Any Other Essentials The five Ws are—who, what, where, when, why and any other essentials such as how. These questions, if properly answered, will cover all aspects of the subject matter. For example, if you are announcing an event being organised by your office, you should make clear what is being done, why it is being done, where and when will it be done, who will participate, how selections will be made, and how entry to the event will be regulated.

3.3 Clarity

3.3.1 Clarity means getting your message across so the reader will understand what you are trying to convey. The need for clarity arises because your reader is not present, and in some cases may not be even known to you. In face-to-face conversation, you may repeat, backtrack, expand, and so on. Incomplete and even ungrammatical utterances may pass unnoticed. But in writing, you have to ensure that the text can be interpreted on its own without any other help from the writer. Therefore, put yourself in your reader's shoes as you re-read each sentence, and see whether your reader will interpret your words and sentences with the same meaning you have in mind.

For making your message clear:

* choose short, familiar, conversational words
* keep your sentences short

* achieve appropriate readability
* put action in your verbs
* be concrete, not abstract

3.3.2 Choose Short, Familiar, Conversational words If you have a choice between a long word and a short one, use the short one. Avoid technical and business jargon, whenever possible, when you write to a person who is not acquainted with such words. Write at the reader's level of understanding. For example, see the following unfamiliar words and their equivalent familiar words:

Unfamiliar	Familiar
Aggregate(adj.)	Total
Consequence	Result, Outcome
Discrepancy	Difference
Precarious	Unsafe, Uncertain
Rescind	Cancel, Repeal

3.3.3 Keep Your Sentences Short In general, sentences should be no more than 15 to 20 words. Longer sentences are difficult to read easily and write correctly. They often slow readers down and may even put them off. On the other hand, too many very short sentences will make your writing sound choppy or childish. So sentence length should be varied.

To keep your sentences short, put only one major idea into one sentence. When a sentence exceeds 40 words, try to write it in more than one sentence.

3.3.4 Achieve Appropriate Readability It means that the word-and-sentence level is appropriate for your readers' general educational level. For this purpose, try to write, as far as possible, short sentences and keep the number of hard words (words with three syllables or more) to the minimum.

3.3.5 Put Action in Your Verbs A verb is a word or phrase showing an action, event or state. It is in active voice when its subject is the doer of the action; it is in passive voice when the subject receives the action of the verb and does not perform the action. For example:

Active Voice: The State Administration coordinated the work of various NGOs.

Passive Voice: The work of various NGOs was coordinated by the State Administration.

You should make your sentences come alive by using the active voice. The active version is more straightforward and informative. Writing in passive voice makes you sound ineffectual. It shows an unwillingness to take responsibility for your action or to assign responsibility to others.

Why do people write in passive voice? One reason is that they try to avoid using personal pronouns like <u>we</u> and <u>you</u>. By using personal pronouns, they will write in active voice. Another reason is that people start in passive voice and then just stay there. They could have easily written the same idea in active voice.

Is passive voice ever right? Of course, passive voice is not always bad. Sometimes you will want to use the passive voice as, for example:

* when you don't know the actor. (The woman was assaulted)
* when the actor is unimportant. (The legislator was re-elected)
* when the emphasis is clearly not on the actor but on the acted upon. (What happened to the school? It was granted recognition.)
* when you want to avoid personal, blunt accusations or commands. (Attendance in the meeting is requested.)

3.3.6 Be Concrete, Not Abstract Abstract writing is vague and general. It leads to uncertainty, misunderstanding, and confusion. It makes readers to guess what the writer means. And even after that, they may not be sure they have got what the writer means. Such writing loses its effectiveness. Concrete words, on the other hand, are specific, definite, and vivid. For example:

<u>**Abstract**</u> A large number of respondents believe that a majority of road accidents are caused by drivers with poor driving skills.

<u>**Concrete**</u> Seventy-five per cent of respondents believe that 55 percent of road accidents are caused by drivers with poor driving skills.

Whenever possible, choose concrete words to express your ideas. Abstract writing is open to many interpretations and potentially inaccurate. Therefore, make a real effort to clarify your ideas so that the reader understands your intention.

<u>How Can You Be Concrete</u>? You can be concrete in three ways:

* use "such as" statements
* tell brief stories
* make comparisons

A "such as" statement is a quick example (normally fairly short—from a word to a couple of sentences). For example:

> **Abstract:** The State machinery should provide immediate relief to the victims of natural catastrophic events.
>
> **Concrete:** The State machinery should provide immediate relief to the victims of natural catastrophic events, such as, organise rescue operations, and channelise available human power into areas where they can be used more effectively.

"Such as" statements make the writing clearer. It is not necessary to use the words "such as" where quick examples are immediately given in bulleted lists. The transitions (or words like them) — for example and for instance—and specific facts and figures make the writing more concrete.

When you tell brief stories, your readers perk up. You also communicate your ideas effectively. If you make them as the characters of the story, they can immediately relate to the situation.

Comparisons do help to make the point. For example, you may compare the technology of the machine you bought a decade back with the technology available now, and discuss the benefits of the new technology.

3.4 Conciseness

3.4.1 Conciseness means you should be brief and to the point, expressing much in a few words. Conciseness contributes to emphasis. By eliminating unnecessary words, you help make important ideas stand out.

To achieve conciseness:

* eliminate wordy expressions
* include only relevant statements
* avoid unnecessary repetition

3.4.2 Eliminate Wordy Expressions You should weed out any words or phrases that do not contribute to the readers' understanding. You should:

* use single-word substitutes instead of phrases, whenever possible, without changing meaning. For example, instead of "for the reason that", say "since" or "because."

* omit trite, unnecessary expressions, such as "allow me to say," "please be advised."
* omit "which" and "that" clauses, whenever possible. For example, instead of "The manager bought desks that are of executive type," say, "The manager bought executive type desks."
* avoid overusing "It is," "It was," "There is," "There are," There were," at the beginning of sentences. For example, instead of "There are four rules to be observed," say, "Four rules should be observed."

3.4.3 Include Only Relevant Statements: The effective, concise message should omit not only unnecessarily wordy expressions, but also irrelevant material. To be sure that you include only relevant facts:

* stick to the purpose of the message
* prune irrelevant words and rambling sentences
* omit information obvious to the reader; do not repeat at length what that person has already told you
* avoid long introductions, unnecessary explanations, excessive adjectives and prepositions, pompous words, and excessive politeness
* get to the point tactfully and concisely

3.4.4 Avoid Unnecessary Repetition Sometimes repetition is necessary for emphasis. But when the same thing is said two or three times without reason, the message becomes wordy and boring. To avoid unnecessary repetition:

* use a shorter name after you have mentioned the long one once
* use pronouns or initials rather than repeat long names
* cut out all needless repetition of phrases and sentences

3.5 Coherence

3.5.1 Coherence means linking sentences and paragraphs so that the ideas clearly express the intended meaning. To achieve coherence:

* stick to one idea for each paragraph
* use transitions and connectors
* use reference words and repeat key words

3.5.2 For coherence in a paragraph, each sentence should be relevant to the main idea expressed in the topic sentence. When you ramble from idea to idea, you lose readers' attention. Most readers prefer to handle one idea at a time. They depend on paragraph breaks to signal the completion of one idea and the beginning of the next.

3.5.3 Transition words and phrases such as 'therefore' and 'however' help point the way from one sentence to another. Likewise, such words and phrases lead the reader from one paragraph to another. These are signposts that help your reader to follow your logic, your flow of ideas. Choose your transition words according to the relationship you want to establish between or within sentences such as, addition, comparison, contrast, cause and effect, sequence, etc. For example, to show contrast you can use words like "although," and "nevertheless," and to show sequence, you can use words like "first," "second," and so on.

You can use coordinating conjunctions such as and, but, yet, or, nor, for, to connect ideas within sentences as well as to connect ideas between sentences.

3.5.4 Link your ideas by referring to or repeating the topic or key words in different forms using synonyms. Use reference words like, this, that, these, those to tie in new ideas with points made earlier.

3.6 Correctness

3.6.1 Correctness means that you should:

* check accuracy of facts, figures, and words
* be grammatically correct

3.6.2Check Accuracy of Facts, Figures, And Words Absolute accuracy is essential for effective writing. When facts, figures, and some words are incorrectly used, they can cause serious problems. So, be continually alert for the accuracy of facts, figures, and of words such as the following to convey the intended meaning:

anxious	Anxious implies worry, whereas
eager	Eager conveys keen desire
between	Between involves two people or two groups
among	Among three or more
continual	Continual means "recurring regularly."
continuous	Continuous means "without stopping"

Your reader expects you to spell correctly, and may question your overall ability if you misspell. Errors of transposition (nad instead of and, and recieve instead of receive) are also errors that show carelessness.

3.6.3 Be Grammatically Correct You should avoid common errors in grammar, such as:

3.6.3.1 Dangling Modifiers: These are phrases that do not logically or clearly modify a specific noun or pronoun. When you can't tell whom or what the introductory word group refers to, rearrange or add to the sentence name of the "doer" of the action immediately after the phrase. Pay special attention to the word directly after the comma and check whether it belongs there. For example:

Lifting the heavy metal desk all alone, a vein stood out in his neck. (When he lifted the heavy metal desk all alone, a vein stood out in his neck.)
After dictating the letter, the mailman brought the mail, which I read quickly. (The mailman brought the mail, which I read quickly after dictating the letter.)

3.6.3.2 Parallelism: In a sentence or a list, present parallel ideas in parallel form. To achieve this harmony and equality of ideas, choose one form of a word, phrase, or clause, and stick to it. Why? Parallel sentence elements channel the readers' attention in the same way as the refrain in a song — there's a familiar repetition to anticipate. For example:

The Administration Department could not decide <u>betweenrental and buying</u> a third photocopier to meet the rush. <u>(between renting and buying)</u>
The agenda for the meeting is as follows: a. calling the meeting to order; b. <u>set the date for the next meeting;</u> c. taking the roll call; and d. electing new office bearers. (b. setting the date for the next meeting)

3.6.3.3. Consistency Sentences and paragraphs should be consistent in tense, in agreement of verb with subject, and in use of pronouns. Consistency assures a logical progression of ideas and helps the reader follow your meaning. For example:

Sometimes a person cannot decide whether they would rather have a raise or a vacation. (Sometimes people cannot decide whether they would rather have a raise or a vacation.)
Each of the day-shift employees go out to lunch. (Each of the day-shift employees goes out to lunch)

3.6.3.4 Logical Comparison When making comparisons, clearly identify the parallels or differences between the things you compare. You can make logical comparisons only between things of the same class. For example:

Our health benefits are different from our competitor. (Our health benefits are different from our competitor's.)

3.7 Courtesy

3.7.1 Courtesy means politeness as reflected in the tone of your writing. It is not mere insertions of "please" and "thank you". To be courteous, you should:

* be sincerely tactful, thoughtful, and appreciative
* omit expressions that irritate, hurt, or belittle
* adopt informal and straightforward approach
* emphasise positive, pleasant facts

3.7.2 Be Tactful, Thoughtful, and Appreciative Sometimes people use abrupt or blunt expressions either because of a mistaken idea of conciseness, or because of their negative personal attitudes. Such expressions are discourteous and you should consciously make effort to omit them from your writing. For example:

Tactless, Blunt	***Tactful***
Your letter is not clear at all; I can't understand it.	*If I understand your letter correctly, it is what you want...*
It is obvious that you have already forgotten what I wrote to you two weeks ago.	**As mentioned in my letter of .... to you .... (date)**

You should show your thoughtfulness and appreciation by sending cordial, courteous messages of deserved congratulations and appreciation. Do not ignore clients' or colleagues' enquiries or requests; ignoring the enquiry or request communicates unfavourable non-verbal message.

3.7.3 Omit Expressions that Irritate, Hurt, Or Belittle You should avoid expressions that offend the reader. Here are some examples of such offensive expressions of such offensive expression:

a. I do not agree with you.
b. You leave us no choice.
c. Obviously you overlooked.
d. You are probably ignorant of the fact.
e. Your apparent disregard of our previous requests leaves us with no alternative....

3.7.4 Adopt Informal and StraightForward Approach Official writing is changing from formal to informal and straightforward. The polite formality of the past is often taken for coldness or snobbishness. The friendlier and more "real" you sound; the better chance you have to relate to your reader. Sentences like, "Should you require further assistance, please do not hesitate to write to me," should better be avoided.

3.7.5 Emphasize Positive, Pleasant Facts You should adopt a positive approach in your writing. That will show that you are cheerful, self-assured, and optimistic. Ideas expressed positively are most likely to be positively received by the reader. It is always more persuasive to suggest what you want than what you don't want, or what can be done instead of what cannot be done. Negative words like <u>no</u>, <u>won't</u>, <u>cannot,never,impossible</u>, trigger unpleasant emotional reactions. For example:

* <u>Do not waste energy</u>(negative)
Conserve energy.(positive)
* <u>Perhaps you won't object</u>(negative)
<u>to my suggestion.</u>
I'm sure you'll agree with (positive)
my suggestion...

4. ORGANISE YOUR WRITING

4.1 You, as a writer, face a challenging task in organising your ideas — putting them in the best order for impact. Logical arrangement of ideas reflects clear thinking and convinces readers about what you have written. Splayed ideas show dis-organised thinking and sound less convincing.

4.2 The Main Point at the Beginning

4.2.1 The key advice on organising your writing is simple: start with your most important and move to lesser important point and then to the least important point. Tell your readers right at the start:

* what your conclusion will be, or
* whatever you want them to do, or
* whatever your main purpose is for the document

By doing so:

* you satisfy all your readers
* your readers will understand and retain information better
* you control what your readers get

4.2.2 Two techniques for organising the writing are:

* the opening statement
* the opening summary

4.2.3 The Opening Statement The opening statement is a sentence or so at the beginning of a document that states your main point. It may or may not be the first sentence, but it should preferably be in the first paragraph.

The opening statement doesn't say only what you are going to cover in your document; it also tells what you are going to conclude, recommend, or request.

For example, consider the following starts of the report by a team of consultants who had conducted a study of systems and procedures in your organization:

After two months` of examining the systems and procedures in your organization, we have found no major shortcomings.

Or

After two months of examining the systems and procedures of your organisation, we have found the following:

* Your Administration and the Finance and AccountsDepartments are following some archaic procedures.
* Your Purchase Department needs to streamline its procedures to remove bottlenecks in the receipt and issue of stores.
* Your Marketing Department needs to adopt moreconsumer-friendly approach.
* There are no major shortcomings in other Departments.

These two starts are better than delaying these findings until the end of the report.

Documents that begin with an opening statement are much shorter. The reason is that in such cases you're less likely to put any irrelevant material. The opening statement keeps both the reader and the writer on track.

Although in short documents it is not as important to put the main point up front as in long reports, but in such cases it is preferable to get the main point early.

4.2.4 Do we delay the main point if bad news is to be conveyed?Two kinds of bad news may be:

* something bad that happened
* a recommendation that your reader won't like

In these cases, use your judgment keeping in view the gravity of the situation and your reader's attitude. You may have to break the bad news tactfully in softer tone. But even in these cases, it is advisable to give the bad news right away. If you are making a recommendation that your reader won't like, or if his attitude is hostile, you may lead up from proof to proposition and lead your reader to the recommendation.

4.2.5 Should you state the main point with facts and figures? A common assumption is that facts and figures speak for themselves, and that any one reading them can draw the obvious conclusion. But the fact is that you need to speak for them. You tell the reader what the facts and figures mean, and do so before presenting them, not after.

4.2.6 The Opening Summary In a short document, the opening statement is a good beginning. But in a longer document, you may like to say more than just a sentence or two. The way to do so is an opening summary.

The opening summary tells in a few sentences what's in the document. It may be the first paragraph or so of a document—giving a complete overview of what follows. It tells the reader what you're going to cover and what you're actually going to conclude, recommend, or request.

5. PRESENT YOUR WRITING

5.1 **When** a document is easy to read and key points seem to jump out at you—that document has visual impact. It appears open and inviting. But if is cluttered, it may leave a poor impression on the reader.

5.2 It is not enough that your writing is clear. It must also have a visual design that entices the reader. Visual design will help your message stand out from the hundreds of documents that are received every day.

5.3 The techniques for having visual impact are:

* use headings liberally
* keep paragraphs short
* use bullets or other lists
* allow for plenty of white space
* underline important steps or dates
* use different typefaces to highlight important information

5.4 **Use Headings Liberally** Headings illustrate in a few words the contents of the paragraph. These are like "labels" for the parts of your document.

Headings speed up reading the document. Readers who are in a hurry can skip through the document and focus on the portion that interests them.

With the help of headings, you can arrange your document into blocks of information rather than scattering ideas throughout the document.

5.5 **Keep Paragraphs Short** A paragraph can be just one sentence or several. But, for visual impact, package ideas in neat paragraphs of six to ten lines consisting of several sentences. Long paragraphs look difficult to read.

An occasional one-sentence paragraph can be emphatic when you want a single idea to catch the reader's attention.

Always start your document with an especially short paragraph which may contain your main point.

5.6 Use Bullets and Other Lists Just as headings show organisation for the blocks of information, bullets and other indented lists show organisation within the paragraph. You may also use hyphens, asterisks, small boxes, checkmark, squiggles, and graphic art (drawing of small pencils, for example) with the help of computer.

If the lists within paragraphs are indented, your writing will be more effective.

When you want to show that the items in your list have a certain priority or order, use numbers instead of bullets or other marks.

5.7 Allowfor Plenty of White Space Whitespace is created by separating paragraphs and sections. It also occurs between headings and text and in the margin—top, bottom, left, and right. White space gives the reader a visual break—relief from the dense look of the text.

5.8 Underline Important Steps or Dates Underlining calls one's attention to key action steps, dates, deadlines. You can use underlining to highlight other important information, such as, vital words, phrases or ideas. Don't overuse underlining; it will lose its impact.

5.9 Use Different Typefaces to Highlight ImportantInformation With the help of computers, you can have different typeface options, such as, bold, italics, all capitals, to draw attention to a word, phrase, or sentence. But do not overuse too many typefaces.

6. MEET THE DEADLINE

6.1 Inmany cases, you may be required to prepare short letters and memos or simple reports of routine nature. In such cases, you may be expert of your subject and be sure of the contents that you may put in your writing. You may, therefore, find no difficulty in organising your writing and presenting it.

But in the case of major writing jobs of non-routine nature, such as, preparation of proposals, project reports, reports of committees etc., you may sometimes find it hard to get started. You may recognize—consciously or unconsciously— that you have to start well, because the beginning of the piece of writing will determine the character of the whole writing. So you may want to start correctly. You may attempt to make a beginning, but you may not be sure of its correctness, and leave it for the next day. The same thing happens the next day, and the next, and, eventually, the time limit comes closer and you are forced to write something, even if it is wrong. How to avoid such a situation? Here are some suggestions:

* plan your writing
* make the false start
* prepare an outline
* start writing
* get distance
* give shape to the report

6.2 **Plan Your Writing** You can make your writing faster and easier if you plan for it. Think about the purpose of your writing, your readers, the information available with you, and the many possible combinations of the beginning, middle, and end, and decide what is the best possible combination of ideas.

6.3 **Make The False Start** So far, you were mentally planning your ideas. But you cannot mentally examine all the possible combinations. You should, therefore, put your ideas in writing in the form of an outline. You can now see your ideas whether they are in the correct order. You will also find that new ideas emerge and the old ideas take a new shape.

By this start, you will also be able to:

* see if the information is complete
* decide what to include and what to exclude
* organize an effective presentation

If you find that more information needs to be collected, do more research, speak with colleagues, consult experts, analyse data, meet with clients, or understand user requirements.

6.4 **Preparean Outline** Outline is the architecture of writing: words and sentences are just the interior decoration. For preparing an outline:

* Put ideas down on pages in random order as they come to you. Use key words and phrases.
* Do not give any consideration at this point to proper order, or separating major from minor ideas.

* Rearrange the ideas in the manner it suits you. Examine one arrangement, then another, until you finally arrive at the one that seems best. Establish logical relationship between your ideas. You can now number them and separate major and minor ideas.
* Use key words and phrases in preparing the final outline. Do not write out the ideas in full sentences. Do not yet think of picking the right words or building into the best possible sentences. Separate your ideas from the words and sentences with which you express them.
* Make your outline a detailed one, containing all of your major ideas. The more detailed the outline, the easier, better organized, and more clearly written will be the finished writing.

6.5 Start Writing: Without regard to style and grammar, write at least one paragraph for each heading containing your major idea. Boldly put your thoughts, even if the sentences are messy and graceless. That can be checked later.

As you write, you will probably warm up; your mind will be focused on your material—more saturated with the information you want to cover. You may discover many sub-ideas you want to mention. Simply re-do your outline as you may need.

Don't get hung up on the first most difficult sentence. If the first sentence is not immediately apparent, forget about it and get on with your writing. You can go back later, when the pressure is off, and put in the missing sentence.

It is a myth that you can produce a perfect draft the first time around. To save time and minimise frustration, simply dive into the first draft with the aim of getting something on paper, rather than trying to get it perfect. You can edit and revise it later.

6.6 Get Distance: If you're close to your work, it is hard to be objective about it. Getting the distance means putting your writing away for a while so that you can come back to it with a fresh perspective. With enough time between writing and reviewing, it will be easier to approach your material as if someone else has written it.

This distance will depend upon the time available to you. It can be a day or two, or more. If that is impossible, then try to complete your first draft just before you leave for the day. Even a lunch break or a ten-minute walk will help.

6.7 Give Shape To The Report: Thereis no one format that is suitable for all reports. But the model outlined below may prove to be useful for most reports:

* **Title** which tells about the subject
* **Executive Summary** which contains the main recommendations or findings, the problem, and what the report covers.
* **Table of Contents** which lists the topics covered and the page numbers on which these can be found.
* **Objectives of the Study** which identifies the problem and the results expected from the recommendations.
* **Methodology** which shows how the problem was approached, the techniques used, and assumptions made during the study.
* **Discussion** which is the main body of the report. It describes the facts collected, analysis made, and opinion formed.
* **Recommendations** which are the suggestions to solve the problem, and reasons for making those suggestions.
* **Costs and Gains** which give an estimate of the costs involved in implementing the recommendations, and the benefits that can be derived.
* **Appendices** which are detailed statements or other information which cannot be made a part of the main body of the report, but which will help in understanding the problem and the recommendations made.

7. CONCLUSION

Always remember that writing is a communication tool of a living society. You, as a writer, should tell as much as possible, as clearly as possible, in as little reading as possible. Develop your skill, and make your writing an effective tool to achieve your personal and professional goals.

EXERCISES

EXERCISE – 1

Fill in each blank using a more familiar word with the same meaning.

1. apprise ____________________
2. augment ____________________
3. consequently ____________________
4. detrimental ____________________
5. endeavour ____________________
6. ensue ____________________
7. incorporate ____________________
8. numerous ____________________
9. remuneration ____________________
10. surmise ____________________

EXERCISE – 2

Rewrite the following sentences with suitable punctuation marks as required:

(a) Supply missing commas

1. The office that he works in is very spacious.
2. Kiran who has never missed a day of work was promoted yesterday.

(b) Replace comma with colon where suitable

3. Make an outline, headline each paragraph, begin each paragraph with a topic sentence, and proof-read for spelling and punctuation.
4. Vacation time increases with the length of service, one week the first year, two weeks the second to the fifth year, and three weeks thereafter.

(c) Replace comma with semi-colon, where suitable

5. The department needs new equipment, however, there is no room to install it.
6. We enjoyed our visit to the word-processing department, moreover, we were glad to meet the staff.

EXERCISE – 3

Think carefully about the function of each pronoun in the sentences below. Put a tick mark on the correct form.

1. Shilpa was clearer than (me, I) about her choice for president.
2. Mr. Anand showed (we, us) newcomers the training film.
3. Among (us, we) executives at the conference, there were many from Chennai.
4. Between you and (I, me), the company seems to be on the edge of bankruptcy.

EXERCISE – 4

Choose the active verb to replace the verb hiding in some of the following nouns.

	Hidden Verb	Active Verb
1.	Be of assistance.	
2.	It is my intention to	
3.	We will give consideration.	
4.	The Chairperson puts her trust in each committee member.	

EXERCISE – 5

Revise the following sentences so they will have active verbs.

1. Final preparations will be made by the planning committee.
2. The result was announced by the Commission on Saturday.
3. These figures are checked by the Finance Department.
4. A decision has been made by the Board of Directors to approve the scheme.

EXERCISE – 6

Substitute one or two words for each item below:

	Instead of	Try to use
1.	after very careful consideration	
2.	due to the fact that	
3.	in a most careful manner	
4.	of a confidential nature	
5.	take into consideration	

EXERCISE – 7

Revise the following sentences to eliminate wordiness.

1. Perhaps may be the chief cause of or reason for obesity in people who are overweight is lack of exercise.
2. These hazards are not visible, and they cause accidents, many of which are fatal ones.
3. When combined together, these ingredients they make a nutritious one-dish meal.
4. Long lines of starving refugees in need of food were helped by Red Cross volunteer people.

EXERCISE – 8

Rewrite the following sentences to make them simpler and easier to understand.

1. The termination of the product line will facilitate the advancement of the company's overall sales.
2. During the course of the week, Mr. Mehra has utilized every available source to locate the materials.

3. Did you obtain a copy of Mr. Sarin's communication requesting all personnel to indicate in writing when they intend to make use of the official car ?

4. Did you sustain any mental or physical injuries as a consequence of the accident ?

EXERCISE – 9

Streamline the following sentences by omitting or changing unnecessary words or phrases, rearranging sections, or dividing sentences.

1. This letter is just a note to be sure that you and I understand what you said would be the criteria for determining the qualifications we are looking for a new programmer for the Computer Department.

2. As a result of a recent meeting I just had with the Personnel Department, I feel it is necessary that I recommend hiring of Ram Gopal for the position of Security Guard, which he seems well qualified for.

3. If the stock arrives without any identification as to whom it belongs to, it can involve quite a bit of time in tracking it down.

4. The critical factor here is to make sure that all the machines that are heavily used are checked not fewer than two times a year.

EXERCISE – 10

Rewrite the following sentences to make them clear and concise.

1. Consumer elements are continuing to stress the fundamental necessity of a stabilization of the price structure at a lower level than at present.
2. Several communications were sent to him instructing him to rejoin duty immediately and informing him that in case he did not rejoin duty, disciplinary action will be taken against him. However, no intimation was received from him explaining the reasons as to why he could not rejoin duty.
3. It is in any case important that senior management should at least involve itself in ensuring the existence of satisfactory policies and procedures for dealing with such matters as recruitment, training and industrial relations.

EXERCISE – 11

In the following sentences, the linking words and phrases are missing. Decide which of the words given would be possible. (In some cases more than one of the words given may be possible).

1. We are writing to you....................clarify certain confused points.

   (a) to (b) in order to (c) so as to (d) for

2. I am sending you my curriculum vitae, as well as other information........ you will have a chance to study it before our interview.

   (a) so that (b) because (c) for (d) since

3. I have had no regular work during the last year............ a persistent illness.

   (a) because (b) owing to (c) for (d) because of

4. I am enclosing a photocopy of the letter............... you can judge its tone.

   (a) so that (b) in order that (c) because (d) since

EXERCISE – 12

Assume that the following words appear in the letters and reports that have been placed before you for signature. Without the help of any source, correct the spelling mistakes in these words.

1. attatched	
2. correspondant	
3. existance	
4. Febuary	
5. paralel	
6. recind	
7. refered	

EXERCISE – 13

Choose the correct word or words from those in parenthesis that should be used in each of the sentences listed below.

1. This act will not (effect, affect) my confidence in you.
2. The discussion (between, among) the five departments has been settled by a (well known, well-known) authority.
3. We sold (fewer, less) brochures last month.
4. A large number of bills (is, are) outstanding.
5. He is not (apt, likely) to gain that distinguished honour.
6. (A, An) university registrar held (a, an) one-hour meeting with the delegation of the staff (counsel, council)

EXERCISE – 14

Rewrite the following sentences that contain dangling modifiers. If the sentence is correct, mark it "Correct."

1. Sounding amazingly like a human voice, she played the flute every day after work.
2. While I was dictating the memo, the dictaphone fell on my toe.
3. When twelve years old, her uncle was promoted as vice president of a multi-national corporation.
4. Unless completely rewired, no engineer should handle this special electrical equipment.
5. Used for only two weeks, Krishan expects to sell his home computer for slightly less than its original cost.

EXERCISE – 15

In the following sentences, correct the errors in parallelism. Mark "Correct" if the sentence is already correct.

1. His typing is fast and he does it accurately.
2. When you make the list, arrange the items in order of importance, write them in parallel form, and all the items should be numbered.
3. He slept through his alarm, missed the bus, and lost his purse, all in the same day.
4. He enjoyed his new job for many reasons: the challenge, the salary, and it was a good working environment.

EXERCISE – 16

Find and correct the inconsistencies in the following sentences.

1. The computer is a time-saving, space-saving invention. They are not difficult to use.
2. Arriving late at work is a problem we all have from time to time. Sometimes we are late because family responsibilities conflict with work responsibilities, and you feel caught in the middle.
3. The typewriter was developed during the nineteenth century. At first they had no shift key mechanism and typed only capital letters.

4. If a reader wants to increase his reading speed, he should first learn to examine the entire book or article in question. He should learn to gather the big ideas in a selection before looking at the details. You should strive to master this technique in order to read more quickly.

EXERCISE – 17

Rewrite the following sentences in a more positive way.

1. If you don't improve your attendance record, you won't be promoted.
2. Do not ignore details; they are important.
3. We regret that we cannot extend your payment date for more than two months.
4. Without proper planning, we will not be able to prevent overcrowding.

EXERCISE – 18

Rewrite the instructions contained in the paragraphs given below to make them clearer and precise.

21. All the incoming mail meant for the University should be received in the Central Registry. The Superintendent of the Registry should open all covers meant for the University, which are not addressed by name to an officer.

    The Superintendent should see carefully whether the enclosures mentioned in the correspondence are available. Any omission or discrepancy noticed should be noted on the letter to which the enclosure relates.

    When the mail is opened, the same should be stamped with the office stamp with date and initialed by the officer opening the same. In the case of a telegram or a fax message, the time of its receipt should invariably be noted along with the date.

22. After going through the formalities as indicated in para 21, the officer opening the communications should pass on the mail to the Receipt Clerk, who should enter the communications in the Incoming Receipts Register to be maintained in the prescribed form (Form No. 5).

    He should sort out the mail branch/unit-wise and register them in separate branch/unit-wise registers. Thereafter, he should arrange the communications in bundles, according to the department to which they relate.

The bundles should be sent to the departmental Inchargealong with the branch/unit register. The Incharge should go through the communications, note his remarks about their disposal, and pass them to the Receipt Clerk in the branch/unit. The Receipt Clerk should acknowledge the receipt of the communications and return the register to the Central Registry.

EXERCISE – 19

The Policy Section of an organisation sent the following note to the Administration Section. Rewrite this note making it simpler, concise, and courteous.

1. We have pleaded with you on quite a large number of occasions to initiate urgent measures to simplify the procedure for handling mail. But probably due to the fact that you are considerably busy, you have obviously overlooked our requests. Accordingly, we attach herewith for your kind perusal the more simplified procedure in order to save time in opening, diarizing, sorting, and distribution of all communications received at the address of our organisation every day. With regard to the revised procedure sent herewith, we would only submit that it has been examined in a most careful manner for a period of a month. In actual fact, we visualize that in a majority of instances it will be found that not only time will be saved, but it will be possible for the concerned branches to initiate faster action on the communications which they in any case have to handle. The chances of errors cropping up during the implementation of the new procedure will be few and far between. Besides, we have tried to build consensus of opinion of user branches.

2. Until such time as the revised procedure is promulgated in your office, the only other alternative will be to provide more staff for faster handling of mail, which you should know is difficult to accept at the present time.

3. We will appreciate your informing us of your point of view in the matter, so that the revised procedure is finalised and introduced from 1st of April, 2022. We expect you not to ignore our request and send your views very early.

EXERCISE – 20

The management of the National Research Institute decided to introduce a system of recording attendance of all employees for better control on their work. In compliance with this decision, the Deputy Registrar (Admn.) issued the followed Memo. Rewrite the memo to make it more appealing and persuasive.

NATIONAL RESEARCH INSTITUTE

No. 14/8/21-Admn. I Date: 15th December 2021

MEMO

Subject: Introduction of Attendance Register

Announcement

1.From 1 January 2022, a system of recording attendance will be introduced in the Institute. It is felt that all employees are not putting in the prescribed hours of work. Many of the employees are punctual, and, in fact, put in extra hours of work. But a few of them are not punctual.

New Procedure

2.Starting from 1 January 2022, each Branch will maintain an attendance register in which employees working in the Branch will record the time of their arrival and departure and put their initials in the columns against their names in the register. The procedure is simple and will take less than a minute each time the entry is made.

Why have attendance registers been introduced?

3.As you know, the Institute has grown considerably over the last few years. Therefore, Management has been feeling that there is a need to monitor productivity and efficiency of employees, and reward them according to the hours they work.

Meeting planned

4.I will announce a meeting with employees soon to discuss the new procedure and clarify any points that they may have.

(ABC)
Deputy Register (Admin)

To
All employees

ANSWERS

EXERCISE – 1

1. inform; tell
2. increase; add
3. therefore; as a result
4. harmful
5. try; effort
6. follow
7. include
8. many
9. payment; reward
10. guess

EXERCISE – 2

(a)

1. The office, that he works in, is very spacious.
2. Kiran, who has never missed a day of work, was promoted yesterday.

(b)

3. Make an outline: headline each paragraph, begin each paragraph with a topic sentence, and proof-read for spelling and punctuation.
4. Vacation time increases with the length of service: one week the first year, two weeks the second to the fifth year, and three weeks thereafter.

(c)

5. The department needs new equipment; however, there is no room to install it.
6. We enjoyed our visit to the word-processing department; moreover, we were glad to meet the staff.

EXERCISE – 3

1. I
2. us
3. us
4. me

EXERCISE – 4

1. Assist
2. I intend to
3. We will consider
4. The Chairperson trusts each committee member.

EXERCISE – 5

1. The planning committee will make final preparations.
2. The Commission announced the result on Saturday.
3. The Finance Department checks these figures.
4. The Board of Directors has decided to approve the scheme.

EXERCISE – 6

1. after considering
2. because
3. carefully
4. confidential
5. consider

EXERCISE – 7

1. Perhaps the chief cause of obesity is lack of exercise.
2. These invisible hazards cause many fatal accidents.
3. When combined, these ingredients make a nutritious meal.
4. Red Cross volunteers helped a large number of starving refugees.

EXERCISE – 8

1. Dropping this product line will improve the company's overall sales.
2. During the week, Mr. Mehra has tried every source to locate the materials.
3. Did you get a copy of Mr. Sarin's memo asking all employees to inform him in writing when they need the official car?
4. Were you injured in the accident?

EXERCISE – 9

1. This letter is to confirm our mutual understanding of the criteria for deciding the qualifications in a new programmer for the Computer Department.
2. After the recent meeting with the Personnel Department, I recommend Ram Gopal for the post of Security Guard.
3. Tracking down the stock that arrives without address can be time consuming.
4. It is critical to ensure that all heavily used machines are checked at least twice a year.

EXERCISE – 10

1. Consumers are stressing the need to reduce the prices and keep them there.
2. Many memos were sent to him instructing him to rejoin duty or face disciplinary action. But he neither rejoined duty nor explained reasons for his absence.
3. Senior management should ensure that satisfactory policies and procedures are framed for such matters as recruitment, training, and industrial relations.

EXERCISE – 11

1. (c)
2. (a)
3. (d)
4. (a)

EXERCISE – 12

1. attached
2. correspondent
3. existence

4. February
5. parallel
6. rescind
7. referred

EXERCISE – 13

1. affect
2. among, well – known
3. fewer
4. is
5. likely
6. A, a, council

EXERCISE – 14

1. Every day after work she played the flute, which sounded amazingly like a human voice.
2. Correct
3. Her uncle was promoted as vice president of a multinational corporation when she was twelve years old.
4. Unless this special equipment is completely rewired, no engineer should handle it.
5. Krishan expects to sell his home computer, used for only two weeks, for slightly less than its original cost.

EXERCISE – 15

1. His typing is fast and accurate.
2. When you make the list, arrange items in order of importance, write them in parallel form, and number them.
3. Correct
4. He enjoyed his new job for many reasons: the challenge, the salary, and the working environment.

EXERCISE 16

1. They are (It is)
2. you (we)
3. they (it)
4. You (He)

EXERCISE 17

1. You need to improve your attendance record to get promoted.
2. Pay attention to details; they are important.
3. You may make your payment in two months.
4. With proper planning, there will be space for everyone.

EXERCISE 18

INCOMING MAIL

21.1. All incoming mail will be received in the Central Registry.

21.2. The Superintendent of the Central Registry will:

(a) open all covers, except those addressed by name.

(b) check enclosures, and note on the mail any omission or discrepancy.

(c) date-stamp the mail and put his/her initials.

(d) note the time of receipt, in the case of a telegram or a fax.

(e) pass on the mail to the Receipt Clerk.

21.3 The Receipt Clerk in the Central Registry will:

(a) enter the mail in the Incoming Receipts Register (Form 5).

(b) sort out the mail, branch / unit-wise.

(c) enter the mail in the branch / unit – wise registers.

(d) arrange the mail in branch / unit-wise bundles.

(e) send the mail, along with the branch / unit-wise register, to the Incharge of the branch/unit.

21.4 The Incharge of the branch / unit will:

(a) go through the mail and note instructions for its disposal.

(b) pass on the mail to the Receipt Clerk in the branch / unit.

21.5 The Receipt Clerk in the branch / unit will:

(a) acknowledge the receipt of the mail.

(b) return the branch / unit-wise register to the Central Registry.

EXERCISE – 19

We have made many requests to you to take urgent steps to simplify the procedure for handling mail. But perhaps due to your being very busy with your work, you have not been able to consider our requests. So, we are sending herewith a more simplified procedure for your consideration. This procedure has been prepared after careful consideration and in consultation with the concerned branches. It is designed to save time in handling both the incoming mail and the outgoing mail. It will also enable the branches to take faster action on the receipts. Besides, its implementation will also be almost error–free.

2. Any delay in the implementation of this procedure may necessitate appointment of more staff to handle the mail. But this option is unlikely to be accepted at the present time.

3. It is proposed to implement the revised procedure from the 1st of April 2022.We shall, therefore, appreciate if your views could be sent to us very early.

EXERCISE – 20

NATIONAL RESEARCH INSTITUTE

No. 14/8/21-Admin I   Date: 15th December 2021

MEMO

Subject: Introduction of new attendance system

Changing needs

1. Over the years, the Institute has worked on a system of trust. The number of employees was small and we could easily see who was and who was not present. Now, because of our growth during the recent years, it has become difficult to keep a track of employees and the hours they work.

Why do we need more accurate records?

2. Management has been feeling that there is a need to monitor productivity and efficiency of employees and reward them according to the hours they work.

New attendance system starts next month

3. From 1st January 2022, each Branch will maintain an attendance register in which employees working in the Branch will record the time of their arrival and departure, and put their initials in the columns against their name in the Register. The procedure is simple and will take less than a minute each time the entry is made.

Meeting planned

4. I will announce a meeting with employees soon to discuss the new procedure and clarify any point that you may have.

(ABC)
Deputy Registrar (Admin)

To

All employees

Chapter - Three

PROCESSING OF CASES IN OFFICE

---

1. INTRODUCTION

1.1 In organizations, a number of documents and information in various forms are received, sorted out, classified, brought out on physical or digital files, examined, submitted with notes and draft replies and after approval, final communications are issued by the staff. Processing of cases in office comprises all these activities. Noting and drafting are important part of this process. The quality of notes and drafts impacts the effectiveness and efficiency of the organization. These aspects, we shall take up in latter chapters. In this chapter, we shall confine our discussion to the processing of cases in the office.

2. RECEIPT AND DISTRIBUTION OF COMMUNICATIONS (DAK)

2.1 All communications (dak) whether in physical or digital form are to be received in the Central Registration Unit (CRU) or the Information Facilitation Centre (IFC). All physical receipts irrespective whether the organisation is working in physical or electronic mode are to be received through e-office in Receipt Index of the Receipt Section. These are to be registered by generating non-editable unique numbers in prescribed form (Appendix I, Page 72). Physical registers need not be maintained in the electronic environment as the system saves all the data and search and retrieval processes are done based on these data: computer number/ receipt number/ keywords/ subject.

> ***E-file***
>
> ***Physical receipts in e-file system are to be scanned and put to the electronic system.***

2.2 Receipts are sorted branch/ section wise and sent to the concerned branches/ section which further distributes these to the concerned dealing hands.

3. SORTING DOCUMENTS BY DEALING HANDS ACCORDING TO FILE CLASSIFICATION

3.1 After a dealing hand receives documents for processing, he should take the action as follows:

(i) Go through the documents and separate urgent ones from the rest.

(ii) Enter all the documents in the Assistant's Diary (Appendix – II, Page 73).

> ***E-file***
>
> ***In e-file, the dealing hand will enter the document in the Assistant's Diary provided in the system.***

(iii) Check enclosures and if anyone is found missing, initiate action to obtain it.

(iv) See whether any other Section / Branch is concerned with a document, and, if so, send copies or relevant extracts to that Section / Branch for taking necessary action.

(v) Take out urgent documents for dealing with first.

(vi) Sort out the documents according to the file classification and numbering system in use in the office.

3.2 File Classification and Numbering Systems

The two main file classification and numbering systems generally in use in offices are:

(i) Functional file classification and numbering system.

(ii) Subject-wise file classification and numbering system.

The salient features of these systems are described in the following paragraphs.

3.3 Functional file classification and numbering system

3.3.1 In this system the range and dimensions of the subjects falling under the scope of business allocated to an organization are analysed in the following sequence:

(a) the main functions of the organization;

(b) the activities in each of these functions;

(c) the aspects or operations involved in each of these activities; and

(d) the factors to be taken into consideration relating to each of these aspects or operations.

3.3.2 The scope of business of an organization is thus analysed under four hierarchical divisions and accordingly the following four standard lists of headings are prepared:

(a) functional heads which may be called 'basic heads';

(b) activity heads which may be called 'primary heads' as related to each functional head;

(c) aspect or operation heads which may be called 'secondary heads' as related to activity heads; and

d) factor heads which may be called 'tertiary heads'.

3.3.3 Based upon the above lists of heads, a functional classification of files for the various substantive subjects dealt with by an organization,together with an identifying file numbering system, is then developed in the following sequence:

(a) A single letter or a group of 2-3 letters, or a Roman numerical representing the basic head followed by a hyphen as a separator;

(b) A 2-digit group of Arabic numerals, (beginning with 11 and continuing in consecutive order up to 99) representing primary head followed by zero as the separator;

(c) A 2-digit group of Arabic numerals, (beginning with 11 and continuing in consecutive order up to 99), identifying the secondary head followed by a slant stroke as the separator;

(d) Serial number of the file opened during the year under the secondary head, followed by a slant stroke as the separator;

(e) A 4-digit number representing the year, followed by a hyphen as the separator;

(f) A group of abbreviating letters representing Section / Branch.

For example, suppose F.No. IV-13024/5/2022-LRI is a file relating to a strike in colliery X, opened by Labour Relations (LR) I Section during the year 2022. In this file number:

IV - is the basic head "Labour Relations";

13 - is the primary head "Strikes";

0 - is the separator;

24 - is the secondary head "Coal Mines";

5 - is the serial number of the file opened during the year under the secondary head "Coal Mines" to describe the colliery involved;

2022-is the year of opening the file; and

LRI- is the Section concerned.

3.3.4 Functional file numbering system for ten functions common to all ministries and Departments has been developed by the Department of Administrative Reforms and Public Grievances (DARPG) with the codes given below:

A	Establishment
B	Welfare
C	Vigilance
D	Common Office Services
E	Hindi
F	Public Relations
G	Finance, budget, cash and accounts
H	Parliament matters
I	RTI matters
J	Electronic Records

These are available at https://darpg.gov.in/sites/default/files/RRS_WC.pdf

3.4 Subject-wise file classification and numbering system

(i) In this system, each Section / Branch should maintain approved lists of:

(a) standard heads, i.e. main subject headings concerning it; and

(b) standard sub-heads, i.e. aspects of the main subject headings.

(ii) The standard heads should bear consecutive serial numbers. No such numbers, however, should be allotted to standard sub-heads.

(iii) The lists of standard heads and sub-heads should be reviewed at the beginning of each year and revised, if necessary, with the approval of the Branch Officer concerned. The serial numbers once allotted to the standard heads should not ordinarily be changed.

(iv) Every file should be assigned a file number which should consist of:

(a) the serial number allotted to the standard head;

(b) the serial number of the file opened during the year under the standard head;

(c) the year of opening the file (all four digits i.e., 2021, 2022, etc.); and

(d) an abbreviated symbol identifying the Section / Branch.

(v) The first three elements in the file number should be separated from one another by a slant stroke and the last two by a dash. Thus, files opened in, say, Scientific Research Section during 2022 under the standard head bearing serial number '3', will be numbered consecutively as 03/01/2022-SR, 03/02/2022-SR and so on, where 'SR' represents the Section / Branch. Movement of Files is recorded in File Movement Register (See Appendix IV, Page 53)

E-file

File number in e-file is based on the type of file numbering system adopted by the Department. In case of functional file system, e-file has a provision to include basic, primary, secondary and tertiary heads in respect of the substantive functions of the Department. E-file also has provision for the numbering system based on subject classification. However, efforts are to be made by each Department to move from the file numbering system based on subject classification to the functional file numbering system.

3.5 File Register

A record of files opened during a calendar year should be kept in a File Register (Appendix III, Page74). A list of approved standard heads along with the serial numbers identifying them should be pasted at the beginning of the register. The pages allotted to the standard heads in the register should also be shown against each standard head. Movement of files be madein File Movement Register (Appendix IV, Page 76). File number should be printed on the file cover in Bar Code.

4. BRINGING DOCUMENTS ON FILE

4.1 Instances where files need not be opened

Normally, no new file should be opened for dealing with documents of a temporary or routine nature, such as requests for supply of unclassified factual information, notices of holidays, miscellaneous circulars, hotel reservations, simple acknowledgements, which:

(i) can be disposed of straightaway by noting the reply on the source receipts or on form letters, and returning them to the originators; or

(ii) are unlikely to generate further correspondence and therefore can be placed in a 'miscellaneous' file which may be weeded out at the end of the year; or

(iii) placed in the folder of circulars etc., if available on the subject.

Officers may put some mark or code to indicate their life such papers. For this purpose, a special stamp with the marks or the codes may be used; it may be combined with date-stamp so that marking becomes easy.

4.2 Bringing the document on a current file

The dealing hand should check with the help of the file register or index slips (Appendix VIII, pages 58-60) whether a file on the subject matter already exists. If it does, this file should be located and the document brought on it. The file number should be shown in col. 4 of the Assistant's Diary against the entry of the document in this Diary.

E-file

In e-file, the file number should be entered in Assistant's Diary.

4.3 Part File

4.3.1 If the main file on a subject is not likely to be available for some time because it is under process and it is necessary to process a fresh receipt or a note without waiting for its return, a part file bearing the same number and the same subject title may be opened to deal with it. This device may also be used where it is desired to consult simultaneously two or more Sections or officers and it is necessary for each of them to see the receipt noted upon.

4.3.2 A part file should normally consist of:

(a) the document or the note dealt with; and

(b) notes and correspondence relating thereto.

4.3.3 Where two or more part files are opened, each should be identified by a distinct number, e.g., "Part File I", "Part File II", and so on. For example, F No. A-12026/03/2022-AdmnI-(PF-I), F No. A-12026/03/2022-Admn. I-(PF-II)

4.3.4 Part file should be merged with the main file as soon as possible, duplicate papers, if any, being removed.

E-file

In e-file, the part file is opened against a main file by any user if he/she is in the channel of submission of that file. Unlike the merger of physical files, in e-file, part file is attached as separate entity and subsequently the respective part files are closed.

4.4 Bringing document on a new file

4.4.1 Title of File: Before opening a new file, the dealing hand should ascertain the standard head to which the paper under consideration relates. He should then propose a suitable title of the file for the approval of the Section Officer / Superintendent. The title should consist of:

(a) standard head;

(b) sub-head which should be more indicative of the precise subject than the 'head', (where it is necessary to have more than one sub-head in a title, the general should usually precede the specific); and

(c) a brief content indicating the question or issue under consideration in relation to the standard head and sub-head and, where necessary, the specific institution, person, place, or thing involved.

4.4.2 The title should be as brief as possible but should give at a glance sufficient indication of the contents of the file so as to serve as an aid to its identification. It should be articulated, i.e. broken up into components, each consisting of the minimum possible substantive words and expressing an element in the subject matter. Each part should begin with a capital letter and should be separated from the preceding one by a bold dash.

4.4.3 Separate file for each distinct subject – As far as possible, there should be a separate file for each distinct aspect of the subject. The title of a file should not be worded in very general or wide terms which might attract large number of documents on different aspects of the matter, thereby making the file unwieldy.

4.4.4 If the issue raised in a fresh document or in the note on a current file goes beyond the original scope, a new file may be opened to deal with it, after placing the relevant extracts or copies thereon.

4.4.5 File Number - The file should now be allotted a number in accordance with the scheme of file classification and numbering system followed in the organization. This number should be noted in the file register as well as on the file cover. It should also be shown in Col. 4 of the Assistant's Diary against the entry of the document in this diary.

4.4.6 File Cover - The file cover should be selected keeping in view the size, type of documents (sheets of paper, booklet's, bulky documents), their likely frequency of reference, approximate retention period, and the possibility of receiving additional documents on the subject later on. The choice of cover will also depend on its appearance, strength, ease of handling, speed of access, storage capacity, and costs. In case the documents are of a transient nature, an economical and simple way can be fastening them to a stiff face sheet, or putting them in thick paper or thin cardboard folders.

4.4.6.1 Files will be opened using the specimen given in Appendix V and VI, Pages 78-79.

4.4.6.2 File covers will be in different colours allotted to different departments / sections for easy identification.

4.4.6.3 If the file contains information of top secret, secret or confidential nature, it will display this fact on the first page of the file cover. Such a file will be kept in safe custody.

4.4.6.4 Instructions for filling the various spaces/cages on the file cover are given at Appendix VII, Page 81.

4.4.6.5 Section Officer will ensure that the various cages / spaces provided in the file cover are properly filled in with appropriate information by the dealing hands in his Section.

4.5 Indexing of Files

4.5.1 Files will be indexed at the time of their opening. Files of purely temporary nature, which are to be destroyed after a year, will not be indexed.

4.5.2 While preparing a title of a file, the dealing hand will underline:

(a) the 'index head', i.e. the standard head or the most important catch-word in the standard head which will naturally occur to any official searching for the file and which will determine the position of the relevant index slip in the consolidated index; and

(b) the 'index sub-head', i.e., the catch word or catch-words in the standard sub-heads and/or the 'content' of the 'title' which will give a further and more specific clue to the file under search.

4.5.3 Where the functional filing system is followed, files need not be indexed under the functional head, main head, and sub-head for which the classification scheme itself will provide the master index. However, such files will have to be indexed under the catch-words used in the content part of the title which falls outside the standardized headings.

4.5.4 After index catchwords in the title have been approved by the Section Officer, the Record Clerk will:

(a) type out, in duplicate, as many index slips as there are index heads and catch-words underlined in the title;

(b) distinguish the index heads from the catch-words by typing the former in capital letters;

(c) indicate at the top of the index slips all the heads and catch-words mentioned in the title, one below the other, followed by the complete title of the file and file number, as per specimens in Appendix VIII, Pages 83-85;

(d) allot a pair of slips to each index head and catch-words by scoring out entries relating to the others as per specimens in Appendix VIII, Pages 83-85;

(e) arrange the index slips in two sets, one in alphabetical order of the heads/ catch-words for use in the section, and the other in the sequence of the numbers for the use of the compiler of the corporate index;

(f) keep each set of paper index slips in separate spring clip folders for each year; and

(g) indicate the date of indexing on the file cover.

4.5.5 Index slips will normally be typed on good quality paper. In the case of important files requiring frequent and urgent reference, however, card indexes could also be prepared. Even here, the duplicate set meant for incorporation in the corporate index will be typed on good quality paper. Card indexes, where maintained, will be kept according to an alphabetical order of their respective catch-words, in a single series for all the years.

4.5.6 Custody of Index Slips/Cards

4.5.6.1 Index slips/cards will remain in the custody of the Record Clerk.

4.5.6.2 After all the files relating to a year have been recorded, the set of index slips/cards in respect of that year meant for use within the section, (viz., that arranged in alphabetical order) will be neatly stitched and the stitched compilation kept at a convenient place for reference by all concerned.

4.6 Inserting document in file

4.6.1 When inserting papers in the file, all pins and clips should be removed, as they catch other material, make the file bulky on one side, and hurt the fingers. If some documents are to be kept together, they should be stapled on the vertical edge in the top left-hand corner. While stapling, it should be ensured that papers are properly aligned.

4.6.2 If a document is torn, it should be repaired withcello tape, lest the torn portion should get lost.

4.6.3 The documents which are ready for insertion into the files should be punched. Depending upon the file cover being used, it can be single punch at the left hand top corner through which a two-pronged brass paper fastener or a tag may be passed. Or, it can be with two holes on the left hand margin through which two metal strips about three inches apart projecting from the back are passed. Another device is to punch two holes in the middle of the left side margin of the file cover as well as the papers to be filed therein and passing a lace fitted with metallic casing at the ends through the punched holes and tying it up with bow knot. The purpose is to keep the filed papers secure and prevent file covers from getting torn.

4.7 Filing of papers

4.7.1 Filing of papers means placing PUC and/or FRs in the correspondence portion and the notes in the notes portion of the file.

4.7.2 Both 'notes portion' and 'correspondence portion' should be placed in a single cover. (In some organizations, separate file covers are used for 'notes' and 'correspondence'.) Left side of tag in the 'notes portion' should be tagged onto the left side of the file cover and right side of the tag should remain as such i.e. untagged. In the case of 'correspondence portion', right side of tag should be tagged onto the right side of the same file cover and left side of the tag should remain as such i.e., untagged.

4.7.3 'Notes' should be filed from left to right in chronological continuous series. Papers in 'correspondence' portion should also be filed in chronological order in a separate series, but the direction in which they may be filed depends on the convenience of the users. These papers may be filed either from left to right (called the 'book form') or from right to left, called the 'reverse book form'. In the first case, the earliest paper is on the top of the 'correspondence' portion and the latest at the bottom, and in the second case, the latest paper is on the top of the 'correspondence' portion, and the earliest paper at the bottom.

4.7.4 Earlier communications referred to in the receipt or issue, should be indicated by pencil by giving their position on the file.

4.7.5 If the file is not bulky, appendix to notes and appendix to correspondence may be kept along with the respective note, portion or the correspondence portion of the main file if these are considered as integral and important part. But, if the file is bulky, separate file covers may be maintained for keeping appendix to notes and appendix to correspondence.

4.7.6 Routine receipts and issues (e.g. reminders, acknowledgements) and routine notes should not be allowed to clutter up the file. They should be placed below the file in a separate cover and destroyed when they have served their purpose.

4.7.7 When the 'notes' plus the 'correspondence' portion of a file become bulky (say, exceed 150 pages) it should be stitched and marked 'Volume I'. Further papers on the subject should be added to the new volume of the same file, which should be marked 'Volume II', and so on. For example, F No. A-12026/03/2022-Admn.I(Volume I). Further, papers on the subject will be added to the new volume of the same file, which will be marked in Volume II, eg. F No. A-12026/03/2022-Admn.I(Volume II), and so on.

4.7.8 In Volume II and subsequent volumes of the same file, page numbering in notes portion and correspondence portion should be made in continuity of the last page number in notes portion / correspondence portion of the earlier volume.

4.7.9 On top of the first page of the notes portion in each volume of the file, file number, name of the organization, name of Branch / Section, and subject of the file should be written prominently.

> ***E-file***
>
> ***In e-file, all electronic receipts including scanned copy of PUC and FRs are attached or uploaded to e-file. For electronic files, the need for creating a new volume does not arise***

4.8 Arrangement of Papers in a file

The papers in a case will be arranged in the following order from top downwards:

(i) Acts/Rules/Instructions or Reference books;

(ii) Notes portion of the current file ending with the note for consideration;

(iii) Draft for approval, if any;

(iv) Correspondence portion of the current file ending with the latest receipt or issue or running summary of facts, as the case may be;

(v) Appendix to notes and correspondence, if required to approve the proposal; else they may be kept in safe custody by the Dealing Officer;

(vi) Standing Guard File, Precedent Book or Reference Folder, if any;

(vii) Other papers, if any, referred to, for example, extracts of notes or correspondence from other files, copies of orders, resolutions, gazettes, arranged in chronological order, the latest being placed on the top. These too are to be page numbered and to be filed in the correspondence portion;

(viii) Recorded files, if any, arranged in chronological order, the latest being placed on the top; and

(ix) Routine notes and papers arranged in chronological order and placed in a separate cover.

> ***E-file***
>
> ***In e-file, papers are arranged in each part of the file as given above. There is no need for Appendix to Notes or Appendix to Correspondence in e-file.***

4.9 Referencing

4.9.1 Every page in each part of the file (viz., notes, correspondence, appendix to notes, and appendix to correspondence) should be consecutively numbered in separate series in pencil on the right top corner. Blank intervening pages, if any, should not be numbered.

4.9.2 Each item of correspondence in a file, whether 'receipt' or 'issue', should be assigned a serial number which should be displayed prominently and in red ink at the top middle of its first page. This serial number should be docketed on the 'notes' portion in red ink giving the following details:

(a) serial number of the communication (on the correspondence portion).

(b) whether it is a "receipt" (incoming communication) or "Issue" (outgoing communication).

(c) No. and date of the "Receipt", or date of "Issue".

(d) the type of the communication – O.M., letter, d.o. letter etc.

(e) Name or designation of the sender or the addressee.

For example, the first communication in the file should be docketed in red ink as follows:

"S.No.1 (Receipt) – letter No. A 11032/1/2021-Est dated 28.12.2021 from the Director General, Health Services, New Delhi."

If an officer has written some remarks on the document, these should be reproduced below the docket, and the note should be recorded below these remarks. In other cases, the note should be recorded below the docket.

4.9.3 The paper under consideration on a file should be flagged 'PUC' and the latest fresh receipt noted upon, as 'FR'. In no circumstances, should a slip, other than 'PUC' and 'FR', be attached to any paper in a current file. If there are more than one 'FR', they should be flagged separately as 'FR I', 'FR II', and so on.

4.9.4 In referring to the papers flagged 'PUC' or 'FR', the relevant page number should be quoted invariably in the margin. Other papers in a current file should be referred to by their page numbers only.

4.9.5 Recorded files and other papers put up with the current file should be flagged with alphabetical slips for quick identification. Only one alphabetical slip should be attached to a recorded file or compilation. If two or more papers contained in the same file or compilation are to be referred to, they should be identified by the relevant page numbers in addition to the alphabetical slip, e.g. 'A'/23.n, 'A'/17.c, and so on.

4.9.6 To facilitate the identification of references to papers contained in other files after the removal of slips, the number of the file referred to should be quoted invariably in the body of the note and the relevant page numbers, together with the alphabetical slip attached thereto, should be indicated in the margin. Similarly, the number and date of orders, notifications and the resolutions, and, in the case of Acts, rules and regulations, their brief title together with the number of the relevant section, rule, paragraph or clause, referred to, should be quoted in the body of the notes, while the alphabetical slips used, should be indicated in the margin.

4.9.7 Rules or other compilations referred to in a case need not be put up if copies thereof are expected to be available with the officer to whom the case is being submitted. The fact of such compilations not having been put up should be indicated in the margin of the notes in pencil.

4.9.8 The reference slips should be pinned neatly on the inside of the papers sought to be flagged. When a number of papers put up in a case are to be flagged, the slips should be spread over the entire width of the file so that every slip is easily visible.

4.9.9 An illustration of referencing in the notes portion and in the correspondence portion is given in Appendix IX and X respectively (pages 86-87).

5. CONCLUSION

Further discussion in the matter will be taken up in the latter chapters on Noting and Drafting. We shall discuss further actions to be taken by dealing hands and section/ branch heads such as examining documents, putting up files, drafting and issuing communications after the decision is taken in the matters.

Appendix – I

RECEIPT REGISTER

(Refer Para 2.1, Page 58)

Registration Number	Particulars of Dak Received				Brief subject	To Whom Sent	File Number	Replied in Hindi/ English/ Bilingual	Remarks* / No Reply was necessary**
	Letter Reference Number	Letter Date	From Whom	Language					
Date of Registration									
1	2	3	4	5	6	7	8	9	10

INSTRUCTIONS

1. Columns 1-5 will be filled at the stage of registration i.e. before the receipts are handed over to the dealing officers.
2. Devanagari script will be used for registering Hindi receipts. Hindi receipts may be suitably distinguished by either marking 'Hindi' in Column 5 or using a different colour of ink.
3. Column 8 will be filled on the basis of entries in Column 4 of the Assistant Section Officer's Register. For this purpose, the Registration Officer will collect and consult the Assistant Section Officer register periodically, say once a week.
4. Columns 9 will be filled by registration officer on receipt of office copy of issue.
5. In column 10, *"Remarks" is filled in based on need by the Section. For instance, 'Movement of receipts marked to officers for perusal' etc. **'No reply was necessary' will be filled in by the Dealing Officer after a decision has been taken at an appropriate level that no reply is necessary.
6. In the case of a desk, all the columns will be filled in, at appropriate stages, by the supporting staff attached to the desk functionary.
7. The Register used in CRU, Section and Personal Section of an officer will be known as CRU Register; Section Register and Personal Section or Staff Register respectively. The format is, however, the same as in this Appendix.

Appendix – II

ASSISTANT'S DIARY

(Refer Para 3.1, Page 59)

S.No.	Diary No. or File No.	Subject	File No.	Date of Submission
1	2	3	4	5

INSTRUCTIONS

1. Column 2 should show 'diary number' or 'file number' according as the paper marked to a dealing hand is a receipt or a come-back case.
2. Column 4 need be filled only in respect of diary numbers.
3. The date on which receipts/ files are received by the dealing hand should be entered in red ink across the page above the entries to be made for the day.

Appendix – III

FILE REGISTER

(Refer Para 3.5, Page 62)

STANDARD HEAD NO. ....

STANDARD HEADING ....

File No.	Subject	Date of		Classification (and year of review)	Remarks
		Opening	Closing		
1	2	3	4	5	6

INSTRUCTIONS

1. Entries in columns 1- 3 should be made at the time of opening files and those in columns 4 and 5 at the time of recording and reviewing them.
2. Year of review in Column 5 is required to be indicated only in the case of class 'C' files.
3. If as a result of the review, a file is marked for further retention, the year of the next review should be worked out and indicated in column 5.
4. When a file is transferred to the department record room or to another Section / Department, the fact of such transfer and the relevant date, should be indicated in column 6. – e.g.:

- D.R.R.	M.H.A.
16-2-2022	26-8-2022

Similarly, when the file is marked for destruction, an entry about the fact and the year of destruction should be made in this column.

Appendix – IV

File No.

FILE MOVEMENT REGISTER

(Refer Para 3.5, Page 62)

SUBJECT

To whom	Date	To Whom	Date	To Whom	Date	To Whom	Date

Space for recording movements of part files

NOTES: (1) Movement will be marked by indicating the officer, section or branch to which the file has been sent with date of sending below it, e.g.

DS(T) 01.01.2022	TRG. 24.01.2022

Appendix – V

FILE COVER

(Refer Para 4.4.6, Page 65)

(To be printed on the first page of the file cover)

NOTING AND CORRESPONDENCE FILE

File No. .... Entered in File Register on ....lume No. .... Indexed On...

CONCERNED DEPARTMENT WITH LOGO

BRANCH.............................. SECTION...
SUBJECT...
.... PERIOD
FROM .... TO .... NO. OF PAGES..............

RECORD OF FILE MOVEMENT

To	No. and Date	To	No. and Date	To	No. and Date	To	No. and Date

Appendix – VI

(To be printed on the last page of the file cover)

(Refer Para 4.4.6, Page 65)

CONNECTED FILES

Previous References	Later References

FILE TO BE SENT TO RECORD ROOM

Closed for Recording on .... To be recorded in Precedent Book Yes/No

Record A (Permanent and Microfilm)/Record B (Permanent but not microfilm) / Record C(To be retained for not exceeding 10 years) / Record D (to be retained for not more than 3 years).

Initials of Dealing Hand .... Year of Review ....

Initials of Section Officer ....

RECORD OF REQUISITIONS FROM RECORD FROM

Date	Requisition		Return Date	Date	Requisition		Return Date
	By	Purpose			By	Purpose	

RECORD OF WEEDING

Date of Review	Action Taken	Signature	Date of Review	Action Taken	Signature

Appendix – VII

INSTRUCTIONS FOR FILLING SPACES / CAGES ON THE FILE COVER

(Refer Para 4.4.6.4 Page 63)

1. **FOLDING OF FILE**

The file cover should be properly folded to create a "RIB". The following information should be written on the "RIB", or stamped by a rubber stamp:

i) File number and subject.

ii) Name of Branch

iii) Name of Section

2. **FILING OF INFORMATION ON THE FILE COVER**

The file cover will have the following space / cages which should be filled in by the concerned section and initialed by the Section Officer.

i) File number and Volume No.

ii) Date recorded in the File Register

iii) Date of indexing the file

iv) Branch and Section

v) Subject

vi) Period From To

vii) Number of pages ________

3. **FILLING OF INFORMATION ON THE REVERSE OF THE FILE COVER**

The reverse of the file cover has been pre-printed to provide space/columns for recording information about details of connected files, requisition of the file from the Central Record Room, and record of weeding so as to watch progress of action in these matters. It also provides the following information about the recording of files:

i) Date when the file has been closed after a review to ensure that no action is pending on any paper in the file, duly initialed by the Section Officer________.

ii) Instructions for recording in Precedent Book ______.

iii) The categorization of record for retention, the date of review of the file for this purpose, and the year of weeding out (in the case of Class C files).

The information about previous references will be filled at the time of opening the file. The information about later reference will be filled when another volume of the same file is opened and at the time of closing the file. Information in other cages and columns will be filled by the Record Clerk in the Branch Record Room / Central Record Room.

Appendix – VIII

EXAMPLES OF TITLES OF FILES AND INDEX SLIPS

(Refer Para 4.5, Page 65,66)

A. Titles with index heads and catch words distinguished.

Sl. No.	Title of File	Typed Index Slips
1.	**2**	**3**
1.	Recruitment of Clerks by Transfer from State Electricity Board.	Recruitment Clerks Transfer State Electricity Board Recruitment of Clerks by Transfer from State Electricity Board. F.No. A-12026/03/2022-Admn.I Room No. 7, Rack No. 9, Shelf 3.
2.	Audit Paras On Corporate Office	Audit Paras Corporate Office Audit Paras on Corporate office F.No. G-25012/05/2022-Accounts I Room No. 7, Rack No. 3, Shelf 4.

Appendix VIII (Contd...)

B. Index Slips as they will appear before they are included in folders

Example – 1

First Slip/Card
RECRUITMENT
Clerks
Transfer
State Electricity Board
Recruitment of Clerks by Transfer from State Electricity Board.
F.No.A-12026/03/2022-Admn.I Room No. 7, Rack No. 9, Shelf 3.

Second Slip/Card
CLERKS
Recruitment
Transfer
State Electricity Board
Recruitment of Clerks by Transfer from State Electricity Board.
F.No.A-12026/03/2022-Admn.I Room No. 7, Rack No. 9, Shelf 3.

Third Slip/Card
TRANSFER
Recruitment
Clerks
State Electricity Board
Recruitment of Clerks by Transfer from State Electricity Board.
F.No.A-12026/03/2022-Admn.I Room No. 7, Rack No. 9, Shelf 3.

Fourth Slip/Card
STATE ELECTRICITY BOARD
Recruitment
Clerks
Transfer
Recruitment of Clerks by Transfer from State Electricity Board.
F.No.A-12026/03/2022-Admn.I Room No. 7, Rack No. 9, Shelf 3.

Example – 2

First Slip / Card

AUDIT

Paras

Corporate Office

Audit Paras on Corporate office

F.No. G-25012/05/2022-Accounts I

Room No. 7, Rack No. 3, Shelf 4.

Second Slip / Card

PARAS

Audit

Corporate Office

Audit Paras on Corporate office

F.No. G-25012/05/2022-Accounts I

Room No. 7, Rack No. 3, Shelf 4.

Third Slip / Card

CORPORATE OFFICE

Audit

Paras

Audit Paras on Corporate office

F.No. G-25012/05/2022-Accounts I

Room No. 7, Rack No. 3, Shelf 4.

Appendix –IX

ILLUSTRATION OF 'DOCKETING' AND 'REFERENCING' ON THE NOTES PORTION

(Refer Para 4.9, Pages69-71)

POWER DEVELOPMENT CORPOPORATION (Ministry of Power) Admn. I Section
F. NO. A-44012/3-2022-Admn.I
SUBJECT FORWARDING OF APPLICATIONS FOR POSTS OUTSIDE THE CORPORATION

Docketing

✓

PUC
P-1/C

References

✓ ✓
Flag A

✓
S. No. 1 (Receipt) – Application dated 3.2.2022 from Sh. Makhan Lal, LDC, Stores Section ✓

Shri Makhan Lal, LDC, Stores Section has submitted an application in response to the advertisement issued by the Staff Selection Commission (Government of India) for recruitment of Junior Engineers (Civil and Electrical) through a competitive examination. The last date for reaching the applications in the Regional Offices of the Commission in 26.03.2022.

2. Shri Makhan Lal is a temporary employee who was appointed on 14.3.2008

2. Vigilance Section have certified that no disciplinary proceedings are pending or contemplated against Shri Makhan Lal.

✓ ✓
4. Shri Makhan Lal's application may be forwarded to the Regional Office of the Staff Selection Commission at Chandigarh. The 'No Objection Certificate' printed on the application form may also be signed.

Sd/-
(Chetan Das)
Assistant Admn. I
10.02.2022
Manager (Admn.)

Appendix-X

ILLUSTRATION OF PREVIOUS REFERENCES IN THE CORRESPONDENCE PORTION

(Refer Para 4.9, Pages69-71)

The Himachal Pradesh Hydro-electric Project Corporation

Sector 17, Chandigarh – 160017

No. F-39/23/2022- Pur

February 12, 2022

M/s Newlook Furniture Works

Haiderpur

Dear Sirs,

Subject: Supply of Office Chairs

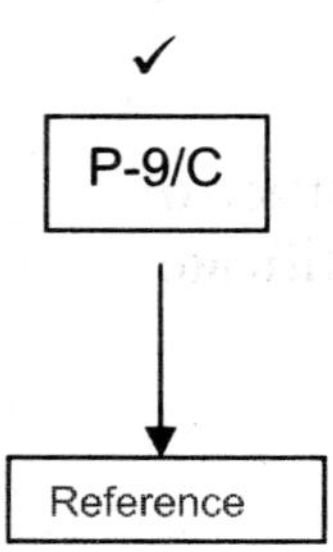

1. Please refer to this letter No. F-39/23/2021-Pur dated 9.12.2021 under which you were asked to supply 100 office chairs within one month as per your offer. We have not received the chairs yet.
2. Please supply the chairs immediately. In case, we do not receive the chairs by January 17, 2022, the order may be treated as cancelled.

Yours faithfully,

Manager (Purchase)

EXERCISES

EXERCISE – 1

Read the following statements and put a tick mark (✓) under the option 'True' or 'False', which you consider to be correct:

	Statement	True	False
1.	On receipt of documents for processing, the dealing hand should separate urgent ones from the rest.		
2.	While examining a case, the dealing hand should check the correctness of all statements made in the document being processed.		
3.	The dealing hand should immediately start processing cases even if the documents are incomplete or the enclosures said to have been sent with the documents are missing.		
4.	The dealing hand should put up a draft reply only after he has been directed to do so, even if the line of action on a document is based on a clear precedent or practice.		
5.	In e-file, the Section Officer will enter the document in the Assistant's Diary provided in the System		
6.	E-office is a digital workplace solution comprising of a suite of products that paves the way for an efficient and open government by streamlining workflow for both inter and intra government processes and making them paperless.		

EXERCISE – 2

Read the following statements and put a tick mark (✓) under the option 'True' or 'False', which you consider to be correct:

	Statement	True	False
1.	The number of levels at which a case is examined should be kept to the minimum.		
2.	The top of the first page of the 'Notes' portion in each volume of the file should prominently show the name of the organization, the name of the Section / Branch, the file number, and the subject of the file.		
3.	While examining a case, the dealing hand should never point out any mistakes, incorrect statements, missing data or information.		
4.	Routine incoming and outgoing documents should always be part of the main file even if they clutter up the file.		
5.	If the issue raised in a document on a current file goes beyond the original scope, a new file may be opened to deal with it after placing the relevant extracts or copies on the new file.		
6.	It is not possible for end-to-end processing of files in the electronic file management system.		

EXERCISE – 3

Read the following statements and put a tick mark (✓) under the option 'True' or 'False', which you consider to be correct:

	Statement	True	False
1.	A file number should be allotted to a file in accordance with the system which the dealing hand may have devised for his use.		
2.	Linking of files is a device for dealing with two or more		

	current files, if the issues raised in them are so inter-connected that they must be considered together simultaneously.		
3.	When filing papers in a single file cover, 'Notes' should be filed on the right side of the cover and 'Correspondence' should be filed on the left side of the cover.		
4.	'Standing Note' in relation to a subject is a folder containing copies of relevant rules, orders etc. arranged in a chronological order.		
5.	File number in e-file should be entered in the Assistant's Diary.		
6.	In e-file, there is no need for Appendix to Notes or Appendix to Correspondence.		

EXERCISE – 4

Read the following statements and put a tick mark (✓) under the option 'True' or 'False', which you consider to be correct:

		True	False
1.	Any number of slips, besides 'PUC' and 'FR', can be attached on papers in a current file so that the references could be quickly identified.		
2.	Routine receipts can be disposed of straightaway by noting the reply on the source receipts and returning them to the originator.		
3.	If an officer has written some remarks on a document, these should be reproduced below the docket on the 'Notes' portion, and the dealing hand should record his note below these remarks.		

4.	The dealing hands should not give any suggestions for alternative courses of action, but merely put up the file for orders.		
5.	A part file may be opened when two or more sections or officers are to be consulted simultaneously and it is necessary for each of them to see the receipt noted upon.		
6.	Unlike the merger of physical files, in e-file, part file is attached as separate entity and subsequently the respective part files are closed.		

EXERCISE – 5

Read the following statements and put a tick mark (✓) under the option 'True' or 'False', which you consider to be correct:

		True	False
1.	Every officer should ensure that cases are examined and disposed of taking the least possible time.		
2.	When a draft is to be put up on a file, it should be placed at the top of the file.		
3.	When putting up a 'PUC' or 'FR', the dealing hand should furnish other relevant data or information available in the organization, even though the 'PUC' or 'FR' does not refer to it.		
4.	Precedent Book is maintained in a Section to keep a record of periodical inspections of the Section.		
5.	In e-file, all electronic receipts including scanned copy of PUC and FRs are attached or uploaded to e-file.		

EXERCISE – 6

Fill in the blank in each of the following sentences by picking up the option, which you consider to be correct, from among those given below each sentence.

1. While putting up a case after examination, the dealing hand should, when a precedent case is available,..........................

   (a) draw attention to the precedent and put it up.

   (b) quote in his note the precedent case in detail.

   (c) refer to the precedent but not put it up.

   (d) ignore the precedent.

2. One of the principles of processing of cases is that the ....

   (a) cases should be thoroughly examined without bothering about the time taken in their disposal.

   (b) paper work should be kept at an essential minimum

   (c) number of levels at which the case is examined should be maximum so that the responsibility for decision is diffused.

   (d) quality of work is immaterial if it is done promptly.

3. It is expected that after examining a case, the dealing hand will write a note in which he will ....

   (a) give a summary of the PUC and submit it for orders.

   (b) keep silent even if the relevant information is missing from the document.

   (c) give his suggestions about the alternative courses of action.

   (d) let the officer find out points requiring decision.

4. When preparing a title for a new file, the dealing hand should ensure that the title is....................

   (a) as detailed as possible so that documents of different aspects of the subject matter can be placed in the file.

   (b) as brief as possible and clearly reflect the specific aspect of the subject matter under consideration in the file.

(c) so worded that no document can be traced without the help of the dealing hand.

(d) so brief that nobody can understand what aspect of the subject matter is being considered on the file.

5. All points emerging from discussions between two or more officers of different organizations and the conclusions reached should be recorded on the relevant file by......................

(a) the officer who is the junior – most among them.

(b) the officer authorizing action.

(c) any officer whom the senior-most officer may ask to do so.

(d) the officer who attended the discussions as an observer.

EXERCISE – 7

Fill in the blank in each of the following sentences by picking up the option, which you consider to be correct, from among those given below each sentence.

1. An economical way of keeping documents of transient nature is to keep them....................

(a) loose below the file.
(b) in an envelope below the file.
(c) in thin card board folders.
(d) mixed up with papers in the main file.

2. When the line of action on a document is based on a clear precedent or practice, the dealing hand should ....

(a) find out new points for thorough examination.
(b) plead ignorance about the existence of the precedent or practice.
(c) wait for directions from higher officers before putting up a draft reply.
(d) put up a draft reply straightaway.

3. If the issue raised in a document on a current file goes beyond the scope of the file.....................

(a) the document should still be placed and processed on the same current file.
(b) a new file should be opened to process the document after placing the relevant

extracts or copies on the file.

(c) the document should be processed on routine sheets which should be merged with the current file later on.

(d) the document should be kept pending awaiting directions from higher officers.

4. On receipt after completion of action, the linked files should ....

(a) immediately be delinked after taking relevant extracts and placing them on the linked files.

(b) be kept together for processing in the future.

(c) be merged in a single file.

(d) be stitched and sent to the departmental record room for custody.

5. In e-file, the part file is opened against the main file by ....

(a) the dealing hand only.

(b) the officer examining the case only.

(c) the branch head only.

(d) any user if he/she is in the channel of submission of that file.

EXERCISE – 8

Fill in the blank in each of the following sentences by picking up the option, which you consider to be correct, from among those given below each sentence.

1. If an officer has written some remarks on an incoming document, the dealing hand should, while putting up the document,..............

(a) reproduce the remarks before docketing the document.

(b) reproduce the remarks at the end of his note.

(c) reproduce the remarks below the docket and then write his note.

(d) ignore the remarks and write his note.

2. The technique of writing a self-contained note may be used for ....

(a) dealing with cases which are within the purview of other organizations.

(b) dealing with important problem-solving cases.

(c) recording points emerging from discussions among officers.

(d) diffusing responsibility of the decision-making authority in controversial cases.

3. When a decision-making authority makes any deviation from the existing rules or procedures, he should.......................

(a) record reasons in writing justifying the deviation.

(b) ask his subordinates to give justification for the deviation.

(c) ensure that the decision is quietly implemented so that no questions are asked.

(d) assert that he would make deviations in future also whenever he feels like doing so.

4. When some other files are put up with a current file.......................

(a) the alphabetical slips attached to such files should be quoted in the body of the 'Notes' on the current file, and the mention of their file numbers is not necessary.

(b) there is no need to refer to such files, and let the officers themselves find them out.

(c) the material referred to in such files should be quoted in full in the body of the note on the current file and thus the need to refer to such files should be avoided.

(d) the numbers of such files should invariably be quoted in the body of the 'Notes' on the current file and the alphabetical slips attached to them should be referred to in the margin.

EXERCISE – 9

Fill in the blank in each of the following sentences by picking up the option, which you consider to be correct, from among those given below each sentence.

1. An officer should, in the performance of his duties, normally act..............

(a) according to his likes and dislikes.

(b) in a manner that he gets praise from the people.

(c) according to his best judgement.

(d) in a manner that higher officers are pleased.

2. While putting up a case after examination, the dealing hand should...........

(a) hold back any additional information available in office.

(b) vaguely refer to the additional information available in office, but not put it up,

(c) seek advice from colleagues about the need to furnish the additional information.

(d) furnish whatever relevant data or information is available in the office.

3. 'Standing Note' in relation to a subject is a ....

(a) page in a book for keeping note of important decisions.

(b) set of model forms of communications.

(c) copy from the folder containing copies of relevant rules, orders, etc.

(d) complete background material for review of the existing policy.

4. When issues raised in two current files are so inter-connected that they must be considered simultaneously.........................

(a) these files should be brought at each level personally by the persons dealing with the files and explain the position.

(b) these files should be submitted separately without any reference to the issues which need simultaneousconsideration.

(c) one of the files should be submitted first and the other file should be submitted after a decision on the first file has been taken.

(d) linked together and then put up.

5. If an officer receives oral instructions from the personal staff of the highest authority of an organization and the instructions are in accordance with the rules and regulations, such instructions should..................

(a) be diverted to some other officer for taking action.

(b) be promptly complied with.

(c) be obtained in writing before taking any action.

(d) be brought to the notice of the administrative head of the organization.

ANSWERS

EXERCISE - 1

1. True 2. False 3. True 4. False 5. False 6. True

EXERCISE – 2

1. True 2. True 3. False 4. False 5. True 6. False

EXERCISE - 3

1. False 2. True 3. False 4. False 5. True 6. True

EXERCISE - 4

1. False 2. True 3. True 4. False 5.True 6. True

EXERCISE – 5

1. True 2. False 3. True 4.False 5. True

EXERCISE - 6

1. (a) 2. (b) 3. (c) 4. (b) 5.(b)

EXERCISE - 7

1. (c) 2. (d) 3. (b) 4. (a) 5. (d)

EXERCISE - 8

1. (c) 2. (b) 3. (a) 4. (d)

EXERCISE - 9

1. (c) 2. (d) 3. (d) 4. (d) 5.(d)

Chapter - Four

ANALYTICAL, CRITICAL AND CREATIVE APPROACH TO PROBLEM SOLVING

1. Introduction

1.1 Decision making is a necessary part of life for any organization and for that matter for any administrator, manager or for an individual. The question, however, is rightly raised as to what proportion of these decisions are correct and effective. In the United States of America, it was found during a survey by the American Management Association that on an average an executive took only three out of five decisions correctly. The faulty decisions were ascribed to incomplete background data and improper examination of the issues involved. Condition cannot be different in India. Krish Pennathur enumerates five bases for decision making. These are intuition (sub-conscious knowledge or blind guess), personal factors (inclination, liking, prejudice or belief), experience, knowledge (proven data or assumptions not disproved) and scientific basis (analysis, evolution and evaluation).

1.2 Intuition, especially if it is blind guess, is a most unreliable base for decision making. The experience is something many managers rely on. Experience is a good servant but a very bad master. Experience is the lesson learnt from a specific situation in the past in the context of a given set of resources and environment. Conditions do not remain static. One cannot, therefore mechanically apply past experience to the current or future problems. Experience has to be suitably modified accordingly. Likings and prejudices tend to influence managerial judgements. Decisions must, however, be objective if they are to be effective. In order to have objective decisions, we must use scientific method of analysis, evolution and evaluation. One of the most successful executives of his time, Robert McNamara, once Chairman of the World Bank, had remarked that decisions were easy to make and that he could take any number of decisions provided all the facts were properly analysed and implications of various alternative courses of action were soundly assessed.

2. Systematic, analytical and creative approach

Our approach to decision making is systematic, analytical and creative. It will enable all relevant factors to be evaluated so that sound decisions may be made. Systematic means orderly, i.e., step by step in a pre-determined sequence. It also means a holistic approach, i.e., look at the whole system, not at any part in isolation, but in terms of its inter-relationship with and interdependency on other parts. 'Analytical' means breaking up the whole problem into constituent parts and critically examining all the parts. Creativity means imaginatively generating alternatives and evaluating them.

Systematic or sequential approach follows the steps given below:

(i) Enunciate the problem and the issues involved;

(ii) Collect and collate the facts related to the problem under each of the five factors. The five factors are: (i) purpose/achievement (ii) means, (iii) time/sequence, (iv) place/location and (v) person.

(iii) Critically analyse the problem and examine the facts;

(iv) Evolve alternatives under each of the factors;

(v) Evaluate the alternatives evolved under each of the factors. Select suitable short and long term alternatives for development; and

(vi) Develop comprehensive, alternative proposals.

3. Steps

3.1 Step 1: Enunciate the problem and the issues involved

First step is to introduce the matter and to identify the issues involved. We may ask questions like: What is the matter? What are the issues involved? What is the genesis of the problem? What impact the problem and issues involved have on the various stake holders? Answers to these questions would help identify the problem and define the issues involved. It would place the whole matter in the right perspective for collecting the relevant facts and critically examine the whole issue.

3.2 Step 2: Collect and collate the facts related to the problem under each of the factors

Quality and success of any decision depends on the complete and accurate facts. It is, therefore, necessary that all relevant facts related to the problem are collected and recorded accurately, clearly and concisely. Collect the whole range of facts in appropriate format, which can help understand and interpret the facts properly. Opinions should be recorded separately. History of the case, details of similar cases in the past, related laws, details of relevant rules, regulations, technical, economic, financial, social, human and other related facts must be collected and recorded.

Facts may be collected, recorded and grouped under the following headings:

(a) Achievement– the nature of achievement; what is being achieved?

(b) Means- the various means, i.e. technology, equipment, material, services, finances, methods, procedures and working conditions; How is it achieved?

(c) Sequence or time– the relative position vis-à-vis other activities or actual time; when is it achieved?

(d) Location–exact location of achievement and environmental conditions under which it is achieved; where is it achieved?

(e) Person– the qualifications and number of persons bringing about achievement; who achieves it?

Talk to all the stake holders and record their views on the issue.

3.3 Step 3: Critically analyses the problem and critically examine the facts collected and collated: the analytical stage

After collecting and collating the facts, reasons for all the facts collected must be found out by asking why all the facts? Why this achievement? Why through these means? Why this sequence? Why this time? Why this frequency? Why at this location? Why by this person or why by this group of persons? All aspects of the problem must be approached with a challenging and skeptical attitude. Every detail must be examined logically and no answer should be accepted unless proved correct. Hasty judgement must be avoided. Remember critical examination is the soul of problem solving. Details must have persistent and close attention. Facts must be examined as they are, not as they appear to be or should be, or are said to be.

3.4 Step 4: Evolve alternatives under each of the factors: the creative stage

It is the creative stage. Critical examination is another name to creative thinking or brainstorming. Here one may have to go mad with one's imagination. Generate alternatives with the help of series of questions.

Why not achieve something else? What else could be achieved? Think of an alternative where you may not have to achieve anything at all, of course, without any negative effect. Execute the physical performance the other way round without compromising the ultimate aim, e.g. removing finger off the ring instead ring off the finger.

Generate alternatives by asking questions like could it he achieved with different technology, equipment, material, methods, procedures or under different working conditions?

When else could it be achieved to ascertain whether that activity occupies the correct place in the sequence or not, whether that activity could be achieved in some other sequence or could it be re-arranged? Questions could also be asked as how many times should it be repeated. Could it be achieved at different time or at different sequence or with different frequency?

Generate alternatives for location factor by asking where else could it be achieved. Could it be achieved at different location e.g. in different locality, building, room, hall, different area in the room? Could the environment be improved upon?

Generate alternatives for person factor by asking questions like who else could achieve it? Could it be achieved with different composition of team or with different qualifications or individuals? Could it be achieved by multi-task workers?

This way by asking various questions you will be able to secure a large number of alternatives under each of the factors.

3.5 Step 5: Evaluate the alternatives evolved: the evaluation stage

Study implications for each of the alternatives evolved. Ask questions such as "Is it technically feasible? Is it practically workable? Is it economically viable? Is it financially affordable? Would it be socially acceptable? Would it be good or bad for the humanity? Reject those which fail on any of these tests. The remaining ones may be classified as short and long term alternatives.

It is important to note that not all the governing factors would yield fruitful alternatives. Sometimes, there would be no need to go beyond the examination of the achievement factor, because that may have paved the way for elimination of the activity itself. Sometimes, it may be the means factor that holds key to the solution or it may be the sequence/time factor that accounts for the solution or it may be the location that yields results in the form of reducing traffic and improvement of environment or it may be the placement of the right person at the right job with proper motivation and involvement that brings about startling results. It may sometimes be a combination of two or more that contributes to the development of real solution.

3.6 Step 6: Develop comprehensive alternative proposals

Development is the key link between the evolution of alternatives which are formative in nature and presentation of acceptable solutions. A particular task may comprise two, three, four or more key factors. Critical analysis is carried out first individually for each of the factors and alternatives pertinent to that factor are generated as discussed in para 3.4 above. A set of alternatives generated in one factor might vitiate the effectiveness of alternatives generated under other factors. During development, the interaction of one set of alternatives evolved in the context of one particular factor with those generated for other factors in various combinations are analysed in depth, refined and tested for acceptability. Final selection of most suitable is based on mutual compatibility (their mutual inter-relationship and inter dependency) classified as short term and long term solutions. Short term solutions are those which can be acted upon within a short period, say a year, within the budgeted amount without any approval. Long term solutions are those which may take long time, additional funds to be provided by supplementary budgeting or which may require approval from higher authority/authorities or change in rules, regulations or a change in the statute. The proposed solutions should be tested not only on technical, economic, financial, social or human dimensions but also holistically studying it as a whole system. Cost and gains should also be worked out for each proposal.

4. Case example

We shall discuss the above given six steps with the help of the following case example.

The Central Roads and Infrastructure Development Corporation has its headquarters at New Delhi. It has 1000 employees, 600 in 15 field offices and 400 at the headquarters. The Corporation involves its employees in the decisions related to staff welfare. It has a Staff Council. The Council has 20 members. Fifteen members are elected by the field staff, four by the staff at the headquarters and one is nominated by the Chairman of the Corporation. The Chairman presides over the meetings of the Staff Council. The Chief Welfare Officer is Secretary of the Council.

For some time, the staff has been demanding financial support for higher studies of their children. The Staff Council in its meeting held on May 10, 2023 passed the following resolution recommending grant of merit scholarships to the children of employees with a view to encouraging them to pursue higher studies.

Resolution: "Resolved that with a view to recognizing merit and encouraging children of the employees of the Corporation to pursue higher studies in recognized and approved institutions, the Council recommends that:

(1) The Corporation should grant 10 scholarships to those children of the staff of the Corporation who obtain 90 percent or more marks in the aggregate in the Senior Secondary Examination for Class XII. The scholarships will be granted to children of those employees whose annual emoluments do not exceed rupees five lakh.

(2) Each scholarship will be of the value of Rs. 500 per month. The scholarship will be for a maximum period of five years.

(3) An annual grant of Rs. 5,000 will be given to each student for purchase of books for the studies.

Funds are available in the budget. The Chairman has the powers to sanction on each scheme of staff welfare up to Rs. 5 lakhs each year.

Please examine the above case and prepare a comprehensive proposal for encouragement of meritorious children of the staff for higher studies.

4.1 Case example: Step 1: Introduction

For sometime, there has been demand from the staff of the Central Roads and Infrastructure Development Corporation, Ministry of Transport, Government of India for financial support to the employees of the Corporation for encouraging their children for higher studies. The Corporation has a Staff Council comprising 20 members, 15 members are elected by 600 staff members in the field; four members are elected by 400 staff members at the headquarters and one member is nominated by the Chairman. The Staff Council is presided over by the Chairman of the Corporation. The Staff Council in its meeting held on May 10, 2023 resolved that the Corporation should award 10 scholarships each year to those children who obtain 90 percent or more marks in the aggregate in senior secondary school examination for class XII. Each scholarship should be of the value of Rs. 500 per month for a maximum period of five years. An annual grant of Rs. 5000 should be given to each student for purchase of books for studies. The scholarship should be tenable only for studies in recognized and approved institutions to children of only those employees whose annual emoluments do not exceed Rs. 5 lakhs.

Why the proposal? The proposal is a welfare measure and is an attempt to recognize meritorious children and to encourage them to pursue higher studies. The proposed scholarships and book grant are not intended to meet all the expenditure such children may incur on their higher studies. It will certainly help them in meeting some part of the expenditure. The proposal also reflects feelings that the Corporation cares for its employees.

4.2 Case example: Step 2: Information collected

Information was collected from the employees of the Corporation about the educational and placement status of their children from banks, from institutions of higher education, from departments for the welfare of Scheduled Castes and Schedule Tribes, for the welfare of minority communities and backward classes and for the welfare of women and children. The information thus collected was suitably collated.

4.3 Case example: Step 3: Critical analysis and critical examination

Information collected and collated as mentioned in the case example step 2 above was analysed and critically examined.

It was found that 20 percent of the employees belonged to Scheduled Castes and Scheduled Tribes and another 20 percent belonged to minority communities and backward classes.

About 40 percent of the students passing out of class XII class were girls.

It was found that public sector banks offered interest free education loan to students seeking admission to medical colleges, institutes of technology and engineering, business management etc. in case the annual income of their parents was not more than 5 lakhs.

The Corporation was providing financial support to a large number of institutions of higher education under its corporate social responsibility. These included medical, technical, engineering, management, commerce, law colleges and institutions for computer science and applications. The Corporation has its nominees on the governing bodies of these institutions.

Eight hundred employees were receiving not more than Rs. 5 lakh total emoluments per annum. We looked at the result of their wards of their class XII examination for the last five years.

It was found that about 250 children of these employees were passing out of their class XII every year. About fifty percent of these 250 children were scoring more than 90 percent marks in their class XII examination. Therefore, there were as many as about 125 meritorious students coming out of the school every year in this category. Rarely any of them was going for higher education because of financial constraints. They were joining petty jobs either directly after their studies or after completing some diploma or certificate courses. Many remained unemployed. The situation, therefore, seems to be serious. They certainly needed support for higher studies which could also help them in their career development. Ten scholarships recommended was too small a number. Much more needed to be done.

On critical examination of the information collected from the institutions for higher education, it was found that they were charging on an average fee of Rs. 90,000 per annum, besides Rs. 40,000 as admission charges. The amount of Rs. 500 as scholarship was too small an amount. It was found that requirement of money for purchase of books was not uniform for all the five years. It could be Rs. 1500 in the first year, Rs. 2000 in the second year, Rs. 2500 in the third year, Rs. 3500 in the fourth year and Rs. 4000 in the fifth year.

Critically examining the resolution passed by the Staff Council, we assume that 10 scholarships will be granted every year and that there will be no dropouts. There will be 10 scholars in the first year, 20 in the second year, 30 in the third years, 40 in the fourth year, and 50 in the fifth and also in each of the subsequent years thereafter. The expenditure on scholarships and book grants will be:

	Scholarships	**Book Grant**	**Total**
First Year	Rs.500 ×12×10= Rs. 60,000	Rs. 5000×10=Rs. 50,000	Rs. 1,10,000
Second Year	Rs.500 ×12×20= Rs. 1,20,000	Rs. 5000×20=Rs. 1,00,000	Rs. 2,20,000
Third Year	Rs.500 ×12×30= Rs. 1,80,000	Rs. 5000×30=Rs. 1,50,000	Rs. 3,30,000
Fourth Year	Rs.500 ×12×40= Rs. 2,40,000	Rs. 5000×40=Rs. 2,00,000	Rs. 4,40,000
Fifth Year	Rs.500 ×12×50= Rs. 3,00,000	Rs. 5000×50=Rs. 2,50,000	Rs. 5,50,000

It means that there will be an expenditure of Rs. 5,50,000 in the fifth year and in each of the subsequent years. The Chairman is competent to sanction uptoRs. 5,00,000 only each year. The estimated expenditure will, therefore, be beyond his competence in the fifth year and in the subsequent years thereafter.

4.4 Case example: Step 4: Generating alternatives

Short Term Alternatives

The proposal as recommended by the Staff Council in the resolution passed in its meeting held on May 10, 2023 cannot be implemented as the estimated expenses in the fifth and subsequent years would be beyond the competency of the Chairman. To ensure that the expenditure remain within Chairman's competence, the following alternatives may be considered:

(i) Reduce the amount of scholarships and retain the book grant as proposed.

(ii) Retain the proposed amount of scholarships but reduce the book grants.

(iii) Reduce the number of scholarships and book grants but keep the amount as proposed.

(iv) Retain the number and amount of scholarships as proposed but reduce the book grant on graded basis. It may be Rs. 1500 in the first year, Rs. 2000 in the second year, Rs. 2500 in the third year, Rs. 3500 in the fourth year and Rs. 4000 in the fifth year.

(v) Encourage students belonging to scheduled castes, scheduled tribes, minority classes, backward classes and girl students to apply for admission to the institutions of higher education as free ships are available for these categories of students

(vi) Encourage students to apply for admission to medical colleges, institutes of technology, engineering and business management. They can get interest free loans from nationalized banks if the annual income of their parents is not more than Rs. 5 lakhs. The Corporation can be surety for such loans.

Long Term Alternatives

(i) Retain the number and amount of scholarships but get the powers of the Chairman enhanced to Rs. 10 lakhs per annum.

(ii) Retain the number of scholarships and book grants but increase the amount of scholarships to Rs. 5000 each per month and get the powers of the Chairman enhanced accordingly.

(iii) Get free education for the meritorious children of the employees of the Corporation sanctioned by those institutions where the Corporation was providing financial support under the corporate social responsibility.

4.5 Case example: Step 5: Study of implications

All the first four short term alternatives are likely to be unacceptable to the staff side, because acceptance of any of these alternatives will mean either lesser number of scholarships or reduced amount of these scholarships and or of book grants. Fourth alternative was, however, likely to be least resisted. Under this alternative the number and amount of scholarship remain same as recommended by the Staff Council. The book grant will be less in the first year and will gradually be increased in the following years as was being found to be actually being spent by the students. It seems rational and practicable. The book grant will be Rs. 1500 in the first year, Rs. 2000 in the second year, Rs. 2500 in the third year, Rs. 3500 in the fourth year and Rs. 4000 in the fifth year. The estimated expenditure on 10 scholarships and ten book grants for the first five years and subsequent years will be as follows

	Scholarships	**Book Grant**	**Total**
First Year	Rs.500 ×12×10= 60,000	Rs. 1,500×10= 15,000	Rs. 75,000
Second Year	Rs.500 ×12×20= 1,20,000	Rs. 15,000+2,000×10=35,000	Rs. 1,55,000
Third Year	Rs.500 ×12×30=1,80,000	Rs. 35,000+2,500×10=60,000	Rs. 2,40,000
Fourth Year	Rs.500 ×12×40= 2,40,000	Rs. 60,000+3,500×10=95,000	Rs. 3,35,000
Fifth Year and subsequent years	Rs.500 ×12×50= 3,00,000	Rs. 95,000+4,000×10 = 1,35,000	Rs. 4,35,000

The expenditure will thus be within the Chairman's competence.

Short term alternative V can be immediately implemented. There will not be any additional financial liability on the Corporation. Short term alternative VI can also be immediately implemented. There will not be any additional financial liability on the Corporation. The Corporation will, however, have to provide surety for the interest free education loans to be sanctioned by the banks.

Long Term Alternatives

Alternative (i): Retain the number and amount of scholarships and book grants as recommended by the Staff Council. It would, however, be beyond the competence of the Chairman. The Board of Director would have to be approached for enhancement of the power of the Chairman on this item uptoRs. 10 lakh per annum.

Alternative (ii): The amount of scholarship as recommended by the Staff Council would not help the employees very much. It is too small an amount. The amount of each scholarship should be at least Rs. 5000 per month. The book grant should, however, be rationalized. It could be Rs. 1500 for the first year, Rs. 2000 for the second year, Rs. 2500 for the third year, Rs. 3500 for the fourth year and Rs. 4000 for the fifth year. It will be in the range of the expenditure being incurred by the students these days. The estimated expenditure on the scholarships and book grants as suggested will be as given below:

	Scholarships	Book Grant	Total
First Year	Rs.5000 ×12×10= Rs. 6,00,000	Rs. 1500×10=Rs. 15,000	Rs. 6,15,000
Second Year	Rs.5000 ×12×20= Rs. 12,00,000	Rs. 15000+Rs. 2000×10=Rs. 35,000	Rs. 12,35,000
Third Year	Rs.5000 ×12×30= Rs. 18,00,000	Rs. 35000+Rs, 2500×10=Rs. 60,000	Rs. 18,60,000
Fourth Year	Rs.5000 ×12×40= Rs. 24,00,000	Rs. 60,000+Rs, 3500×10=Rs. 95,000	Rs. 24,95,000
Fifth Year and subsequent years	Rs.5000 ×12×50= Rs. 30,00,000	Rs. 95,000+Rs, 4000×10=Rs. 1,35,000	Rs. 31,35,000

It would imply that Corporation would have to increase the financial provision under the staff welfare head to accommodate increase in the expenditure on scholarships and book grants accordingly.

It would also imply that Board of Directors would also have to increase power of the Chairman accordingly.

Alternative (iii): The Corporation will have to assert itself to get the required free ships sanctioned by the institutions being provided grants under its corporate social responsibility. The Corporation in the bargain may have to increase its grant to these institutions.

4.6 Case example: Step 6: Development of comprehensive proposals

Short Term Proposals

(1) Employees belonging to scheduled castes, scheduled tribes, minority communities, backward classes and parents of girl students scoring 90% or more

than 90 percent marks in their class XII examination should be encouraged to seek admission to institutions of higher education. Freeships are available for the students in these categories. It would cover about 100 out of 125 students scoring 90 or more than 90 percent marks in their class XII examination (20 percent belonging to scheduled castes and scheduled tribes, 20 percent to minority communities and backward classes and 40 percent being girl students). There will be no financial burden on the Corporation.

(2) The Corporation may sanction ten merit scholarships each of Rs. 500 per month for five years as recommended by the Staff Council. It may sanction book grant to each selected student book grant may be Rs. 1500 for the first year, Rs. 2000 for the second year, Rs. 2500 for the third year, Rs. 3500 for the fourth year and Rs. 4000 for the fifth year to each student availing merit scholarship. It would be least resisted by the staff members as the amount sanctioned will be enough to meet their expenditure on purchase of books. Merit scholarships may be awarded on merit to the students scoring 90 percent or more marks in their class XII examination. Their parents should be not earning more than Rs. 5 lakhs per annum. Total expenditure would be within the competence of the Chairman. An amount of Rs. 65,000 would still be left for negotiation with staff members.

(3) Recipients of merit scholarships and the remaining 15 meritorious students should be helped by the Corporation by furnishing surety to the interest free education loans from the public sector banks after admission to medical colleges, institutes of technology, engineering computer science and applications and business management schools. It would enable the merit scholarship recipients and other meritorious students to meet high expenditure on their higher education. Scholarships may not be sufficient to cover the high fee and admission charges.

Long Term Proposals

(1) Increase the power of the Chairman to sanction the amount uptoRs. 10 lakhseach per annum under this head. Sanction the number and amount of merit scholarships and book grants as recommended by the Staff Council.

(2) The amount of each of the ten merit scholarships should be Rs. 5000 per month for five years. The book grant should be Rs. 1500 for the first year, Rs. 2000 for the second year, Rs. 2500 for the third year, Rs. 3500 for the fourth year and 4000 for the fifth year. The estimated expenditure during the fifth and subsequent years would be Rs. 31,35,000. Budget provision under the requisite head may be increased to Rs. 40,00,000 and power of the Chairman to sanction expenditure under this head should also be increased accordingly.

(3) The Corporation should get certain number of freeships for the children of its employees sanctioned by institutions being helped under its corporate social responsibility. The Corporation in the bargain may increase its grant to these institutions.

The above given short and long term proposals will help not only students scoring 90% or more than 90% marks in their class XII examinations but also some others scoring less than 90 percent marks.

5. Presenting comprehensive composite proposal

The developed composite proposals should be presented in a manner which can help competent authorities understand the problem and issues involved and also in taking the right decision. It should be comprehensive, logical, coherent, convincing, concise and precise using all the principles of effective writing and presentation. We have the following brief suggestions:

(i) Introduction: the opening paragraph: Introduce the problem, the issues and stakeholders involved in the opening paragraph. Give brief history of the matter.

(ii) Cite essential facts including rules, regulations, laws, policy, precedents, their important interpretations and other relevant facts in brief on the subject.

(iii) State various possible solutions and their implications from technical, procedural, economic, financial, social and human angles.

(iv) Suggest most suitable short and long term solutions with sound justification and potential impact. State clearly the financial and other liabilities involved and availability of finances and other resources. Mention the competent authority/authorities to take final decisions. Mention if other organizations, departments are to be consulted and at what stage.

(v) Mention if any long term steps need to be taken such as change in the policy or the law.

Incorporating steps, 1, 2, 3, 4, 5 and 6 under respective headings integrated together as given in the case example will form a composite comprehensive proposal which can be presented to the competent authority to take appropriate decision. Such a proposal is given in the note at the Annexure for suitable decision by the authorities.

6. Conclusion:

The above discussion is comprehensive. It is systematic, analytical, creative and dynamic enough to enable every one take quick, correct and effective decisions, both short and long term. In the case example, if the short term and long term proposals are accepted and implemented, then not only ten meritorious children of the employees not earning annually more than rupees five lakh as recommended by the Staff Council, but also all other 115 meritorious children could benefit and get free ships and scholarships.

Annexure

CENTRAL ROADS and INFRASTRUCTURE DEVELOPMENT CORPORATION (Ministry of Transport, Government of India) Admn. II Section
F. No. B-12022/5/2022 – Admn. II
SUBJECT Staff Council's Proposal for Grant of merit scholarships to the children of employees of the Corporation.

S. No. 1 (Receipt) Letter dated 26.3.2022 from the Secretary, Staff Council, Central Roads and Infrastructure Development Corporation.

1. **Proposal** – Secretary, Staff Council of our Corporation, has sent a copy of the Resolution passed by the Staff Council on 23.3.2022 about the grant of merit scholarships to children of employees of the Corporation. These scholarships will be granted to those children who obtain 90% or more marks in the Senior Secondary School Examination for Class XII. According to the Resolution, 10 scholarships, each of which will be of Rs. 500/- per month, will be granted every year. In the case of students in the Arts, Commerce, and Science streams, the scholarships will be for a period of three years initially, extendable by another two years for those students who pursue post graduate courses (including management courses) in these streams. In the case of students in medical, architecture, technical, and law streams the scholarships will be for the duration of the course, subject to a maximum of five years. An annual book grant of Rs. 5000/- each will also be given to the students.

2. **Why the proposal?** The proposal is a welfare measure for employees and an attempt to recognize meritorious children, and encourage them to pursue higher studies. The proposal scholarships and grant are not intended to meet all the expenditure such children may incur on their studies, but it will certainly help in meeting some part of the

expenditure. The proposal also reflects the feeling that the corporation cares for its employees.

3. **Implications of the proposal** - Assuming that in the first year, 10 students will be awarded scholarships and the annual book grant and, as they move up, successive batches of students will be similarly awarded, the total number of students during the five-year period and also during the subsequent years will be as shown below:

1st year	=	10	=	10
2nd year	=	10 + 10	=	20
3rd year	=	10 + 10 + 10	=	30
4th year	=	10 + 10 + 10 + 10	=	40
5th year	=	10 + 10 + 10 + 10 + 10	=	50

In subsequent years, the number will remain 50, as one batch will move out on completion of 5 years and new batch will come in.

4. **The expenditure on scholarships and book grants will be:**

	Scholarship	Book Grant	Total
	Rs.	Rs.	Rs.
1st year	$=10 \times 6000 = 60000$	$10 \times 5000 = 50000$	1,10,000
2nd year	$=20 \times 6000 = 1,20,000$	$20 \times 5000 = 1,00,000$	2,20,000
3rd year	$=30 \times 6000 = 1,80,000$	$30 \times 5000 = 1,50,000$	3,30,000
4th year	$=40 \times 6000 = 2,40,000$	$40 \times 5000 = 2,00,000$	4,40,000
5th year	$=50 \times 6000 = 3,00,000$	$50 \times 5000 = 2,50,000$	5,50,000

and it will be Rs. 5,50,000 in each of the subsequent years. Thus, in the 5th year and therefore the annual expenditure will be Rs. 5,50,000. But, Chairman is competent to sanction uptoRs. 5,00,000 only in each case. The estimated expenditure will, therefore, be beyond his competence in the fifth year and beyond.

5. Information collected

Information was collected from the employees of the Corporation about the educational and placement status of their children from banks, from institutions of higher education, from departments for the welfare of Scheduled Castes and Schedule Tribes, for the welfare of minority communities and backward classes and for the welfare of women and children. The information thus collected was suitably collated.

6. Critical analysis and critical examination

Information collected and collated as mentioned in the case example step 2 above was analysed and critically examined.

It was found that 20 percent of the employees belonged to Scheduled Castes and Scheduled Tribes and another 20 percent belonged to minority communities and backward classes.

About 40 percent of the students passing out of class XII class were girls.

It was found that public sector banks offered interest free education loan to students seeking admission to medical colleges, institutes of technology and engineering, business management etc. in case the annual income of their parents was not more than 5 lakhs.

The Corporation was providing financial support to a large number of institutions of higher education under its corporate social responsibility. These included medical, technical, engineering, management, commerce, law colleges and institutions for computer science and applications. The Corporation has its nominees on the governing bodies of these institutions.

Eight hundred employees were receiving not more than Rs. 5 lakhs total emoluments per annum. We looked at the result of their wards of their class XII examination for the last five years.

It was found that about 250 children of these employees were passing out of their class XII every year. About fifty percent of these 250 children were scoring more than 90 percent marks in their class XII examination. Therefore, there were as many as about 125 meritorious students coming out of the school every year in this category. Rarely any of them was going for higher education because of financial constraints. They were joining petty jobs either directly after their studies or after completing some diploma or certificate courses. Many remained unemployed. The situation, therefore, seems to be serious. They certainly needed support for higher studies which could also help them in their career development. Ten scholarships recommended was too small a number. Much more needed to be done.

On critical examination of the information collected from the institutions for higher education, it was found that they were charging on an average fee of Rs. 90,000 per annum, besides Rs. 40,000 as admission charges. The amount of Rs. 500 as scholarship was too small an amount. It was found that requirement of money for purchase of books was not uniform for all the five years. It could be Rs. 1500 in the first year, Rs. 2000 in the second year, Rs. 2500 in the third year, Rs. 3500 in the fourth year and Rs. 4000 in the fifth year.

Critically examining the resolution passed by the Staff Council, we assume that 10 scholarships will be granted every year and that there will be no dropouts. There will be 10 scholars in the first year, 20 in the second year, 30 in the third years, 40 in the fourth year, and 50 in the fifth and also in each of the subsequent years thereafter. The expenditure on scholarships and book grants will be:

	Scholarships	**Book Grant**	**Total**
First Year	Rs.500 ×12×10= 60,000	Rs. 5000×10=Rs. 50,000	Rs. 1,10,000
Second Year	Rs.500 ×12×20= 1,20,000	Rs. 5000×20=Rs. 1,00,000	Rs. 2,20,000
Third Year	Rs.500 ×12×30= 1,80,000	Rs. 5000×30=Rs. 1,50,000	Rs. 3,30,000
Fourth Year	Rs.500 ×12×40= 2,40,000	Rs. 5000×40=Rs. 2,00,000	Rs. 4,40,000
Fifth Year	Rs.500 ×12×50= 3,00,000	Rs. 5000×50=Rs. 2,50,000	Rs. 5,50,000

It means that there will be an expenditure of Rs. 5,50,000 in the fifth year and in each of the subsequent years. The Chairman is competent to sanction up toRs. 5,00,000 only each year. The estimated expenditure will, therefore, be beyond his competence in the fifth year and in the subsequent years thereafter.

7. Short-term and Long-term Alternatives

7.1 Short Term Alternatives

The proposal as recommended by the Staff Council in the resolution passed in its meeting held on March 23, 2022 cannot be implemented as the estimated expenses in the fifth and subsequent years would be beyond the competency of the Chairman. To ensure that the expenditure remain within Chairman's competence, the following alternatives may be considered:

(i) Reduce the amount of scholarships and retain the book grant as proposed.

(ii) Retain the proposed amount of scholarships but reduce the book grants.

(iii) Reduce the number of scholarships and book grants but keep the amount as proposed.

(iv) Retain the number and amount of scholarships as proposed but reduce the book grant on graded basis. It may be Rs. 1500 in the first year, Rs. 2000 in the second year, Rs. 2500 in the third year, Rs. 3500 in the fourth year and Rs. 4000 in the fifth year.

(v) Encourage students belonging to scheduled castes, scheduled tribes, minority classes, backward classes and girl students to apply for admission to the institutions of higher education as free ships are available for these categories of students

(vi) Encourage students to apply for admission to medical colleges, institutes of technology, engineering and business management. They can get interest free loans from nationalized banks if the annual income of their parents is not more than Rs. 5 lakhs. The Corporation can be surety for such loans.

7.2 Long Term Alternatives

(i) Retain the number and amount of scholarships but get the powers of the Chairman enhanced to Rs. 10 lakhs per annum.

(ii) Retain the number of scholarships and book grants but increase the amount of scholarships to Rs. 5000 each per month and get the powers of the Chairman enhanced accordingly.

(iii) Get free education for the meritorious children of the employees of the Corporation sanctioned by those institutions where the Corporation was providing financial support under the corporate social responsibility.

8. Implications of Short-term and Long-term Alternatives

8.1 Short-term Alternatives

All the first four short term alternatives are likely to be unacceptable to the staff side, because acceptance of any of these alternatives will mean either lesser number of scholarships or reduced amount of these scholarships and or of book grants. Fourth alternative was, however, likely to be least resisted. Under this alternative the number and amount of scholarship remain same as recommended by the Staff Council. The book grant will be less in the first year and will gradually be increased in the following years as was being found to be actually being spent by the students. It seems rational and practicable. The book grant will be Rs. 1500 in the first year, Rs. 2000 in the second year, Rs. 2500 in the third year, Rs. 3500 in the fourth year and Rs. 4000 in the fifth year. The estimated expenditure on 10 scholarships and ten book grants for the first five years and subsequent years will be as follows

	Scholarships	**Book Grant**	**Total**
First Year	Rs.500 × 12 × 10= Rs. 60,000	Rs. 1,500 × 10 = Rs. 15,000	Rs. 75,000
Second Year	Rs.500 × 1 2 × 20= Rs. 1,20,000	Rs. 15,000 + Rs. 2,000 × 10=Rs. 35,000	Rs. 1,55,000
Third Year	Rs.500 × 12 × 30 = Rs. 1,80,000	Rs. 35,000 + Rs. 2,500 × 10=Rs. 60,000	Rs. 2,40,000
Fourth Year	Rs.500 × 12 × 40 = Rs. 2,40,000	Rs. 60,000 + Rs. 3,500 × 10=Rs. 95,000	Rs. 3,35,000
Fifth Year and subsequent years	Rs.500 × 12 × 50 = Rs. 3,00,000	Rs. 95,000 + Rs. 4,000 × 10=Rs. 1,35,000	Rs. 4,35,000

The expenditure will thus be within the Chairman's competence.

Short term alternative V can be immediately implemented. There will not be any additional financial liability on the Corporation. Short term alternative VI can also be immediately implemented. There will not be any additional financial liability on the Corporation. The Corporation will, however, have to provide surety for the interest free education loans to be sanctioned by the banks.

8.2 Long Term Alternatives

Alternative (i): Retain the number and amount of scholarships and book grants as recommended by the Staff Council. It would, however, be beyond the competence of the Chairman. The Board of Director would have to be approached for enhancement of the power of the Chairman on this item uptoRs. 10 lakhs per annum.

Alternative (ii): The amount of scholarship as recommended by the Staff Council would not help the employees very much. It is too small an amount. The amount of each scholarship should be at least Rs. 5000 per month. The book grant should, however, be rationalized. It could be Rs. 1500 for the first year, Rs. 2000 for the second year, Rs. 2500 for the third year, Rs. 3500 for the fourth year and Rs. 4000 for the fifth year. It will be in the range of the expenditure being incurred by the students these days. The estimated expenditure on the scholarships and book grants as suggested will be as given below:

	Scholarships	**Book Grant**	**Total**
First Year	Rs.5000 × 12 × 10 = Rs. 6,00,000	Rs. 1500 × 10 = Rs. 15,000	Rs. 6,15,000
Second Year	Rs.5000 × 12× 20 = Rs. 12,00,000	Rs. 15000 + Rs. 2000 × 10 = Rs. 35,000	Rs. 12,35,000
Third Year	Rs.5000 × 12 × 30 = Rs. 18,00,000	Rs. 35000 + Rs, 2500 × 10 = Rs. 60,000	Rs. 18,60,000
Fourth Year	Rs.5000 × 12 × 40 = Rs. 24,00,000	Rs. 60,000 + 3500 × 10 = Rs. 95,000	Rs. 24,95,000
Fifth Year and subsequent years	Rs.5000 × 12 × 50 = Rs. 30,00,000	Rs. 95,000 + 4000 × 10 = Rs. 1,35,000	Rs. 31,35,000

It would imply that Corporation would have to increase the financial provision under the staff welfare head to accommodate increase in the expenditure on scholarships and book grants accordingly.

It would also imply that Board of Directors would also have to increase power of the Chairman accordingly.

Alternative (iii): The Corporation will have to assert itself to get the required free ships sanctioned by the institutions being provided grants under its corporate social responsibility. The Corporation in the bargain may have to increase its grant to these institutions.

9. Recommendations

9.1 Short Term Proposals

1. Employees belonging to scheduled castes, scheduled tribes, minority communities, backward classes and parents of girl students scoring 90% or more than 90 percent marks in their class XII examination should be encouraged to seek admission to institutions of higher education. Freeships are available for the students in these categories. It would cover about 100 out of 125 students scoring 90 or more than 90 percent marks in their class XII examination (20 percent belonging to scheduled castes and scheduled tribes, 20 percent to minority communities and backward classes and 40 percent being girl students). There will be no financial burden on the Corporation.

2. The Corporation may sanction ten merit scholarships each of Rs. 500 per month for five years as recommended by the Staff Council. It may sanction book grant to each selected student book grant may be Rs. 1500 for the first year, Rs. 2000 for the second year, Rs. 2500 for the third year, Rs. 3500 for the fourth year and Rs. 4000 for the fifth year to each student availing merit scholarship. It would be least resisted by the staff members as the amount sanctioned will be enough to meet their expenditure on purchase of books. Merit scholarships may be awarded on merit to the students scoring 90 percent or more marks in their class XII examination. Their parents should be not earning more than Rs. 5 lakhs per annum. Total expenditure would be within the competence of the Chairman. An amount of Rs. 65,000 would still be left for negotiation with staff members.

3. Recipients of merit scholarships and the remaining 15 meritorious students should be helped by the Corporation by furnishing surety to the interest free education loans from the public sector banks after admission to medical colleges, institutes of technology, engineering computer science and applications and business management schools. It would enable the merit scholarship recipients and other meritorious students to meet high expenditure on their higher education. Scholarships may not be sufficient to cover the high fee and admission charges.

9.2 Long Term Proposals

1. Increase the power of the Chairman to sanction the amount uptoRs. 10 lakhs each per annum under this head. Sanction the number and amount of merit scholarships and book grants as recommended by the Staff Council.

2. The amount of each of the ten merit scholarships should be Rs. 5000 per month for five years. The book grant should be Rs. 1500 for the first year, Rs. 2000 for the

second year, Rs. 2500 for the third year, Rs. 3500 for the fourth year and 4000 for the fifth year. The estimated expenditure during the fifth and subsequent years would be Rs. 31,35,000. Budget provision under the requisite head may be increased to Rs. 40,00,000 and power of the Chairman to sanction expenditure under this head should also be increased accordingly.

3. The Corporation should get certain number of freeships for the children of its employees sanctioned by institutions being helped under its corporate social responsibility. The Corporation in the bargain may increase its grant to these institutions.

4. The above given short and long term proposals will help not only students scoring 90% or more than 90% marks in their class XII examinations but also some others scoring less than 90 percent marks.

It is suggested that short term and long term alternatives be approved. Thereafter, the staff side may also be consulted and their agreement obtained. Further details about eligibility, mode of disbursement, monitoring of the students' progress etc. will be worked out after the agreement of the staff side has been obtained.

10. **Approval** – Chairman's approval to the recommendations above may be obtained. Thereafter, case may be submitted for approval of the Board wherever required.

Sd/- Lalit Narayan

30.4.2022

Supdt. (Admn. II)

Exercises

Read the following statements and put a tick (✓) under the option 'True' or 'False', which you consider to be correct:

S. No.		True	False
1.	Intuition is a most reliable base for decision making		
2.	Experience is a good servant but a very badmaster.		
3.	Critical examination is not the same as creative thinking.		
4.	Critical examination is the soul of systematic and analytical approach to problem solving.		
5.	The right approach to decision making in the words of Russel Currie should be "systematic and analytical approach to problem which will not enable all relevant factors to be evaluated so that decision may be made.		
6.	While liking and prejudices, tend to influence managerial judgements, decisions must not be objective if they are to be effective.		
7.	Generate alternatives by asking questions, "why achieve something else?"		
8.	Hasty judgement must be avoided.		
9.	Facts must be examined as they appear to be and not as they are.		
10.	Development— is not the key link between the evaluation of alternatives which are formative in nature and presentation of acceptable solutions.		

Answers

1.	False	2.	True
3.	False	4.	True
5.	False	6.	False
7.	False	8.	True
9.	False	10.	False

Chapter - Five

FORMS OF WRITTEN COMMUNICATION

1. INTRODUCTION

1.1 Written communication aims at transmitting and receiving messages, and linking various components of an organization, as well as the organization with external agencies. It helps avoid distortions in messages that are relayed orally, and recall past information when necessary.

1.2 Government organizations adopt different forms of written communication to convey their messages. Each form has its use, and in some cases, a phraseology of its own. We shall discuss some of these forms in this chapter. In our earlier editions, we had discussed telegram and telex forms of communication also. In view of technological developments, faster forms have come in and telegram and telex systems are no longer in use.

2. FORMS OF WRITTEN COMMUNICATION

2.1 The main forms of written communication which we shall discuss are:

(i) Letter
(ii) Demi – Official (D.O.) Letter
(iii) Office Memorandum/ Memorandum/ Memo
(iv) Inter-departmental (U.O.) note
(v) Office order / Order
(vi) Notification
(vii) Resolution
(viii) Press communiqué/Press Note
(ix) Endorsement
(x) Circular
(xi) E-mail

2.2 E-mail and SMS have gained great popularity. These are not only accepted, rather are promoted as forms of communication by more and more organisations. We have added a separate chapter on these forms of communication.

2.3 Written communication can be sent through a messenger or a courier. It can also be sent through ordinary post, registered or registered AD post or speed-post. When it is considered necessary to communicate with general public to create awareness about any matter, the form of advertisement through audio-visual or written media may be used.

2.4 Let us now discuss the forms of written communication.

3. LETTER

3.1 **Uses:** Letter is a principal form of communication with external agencies. It is used for corresponding with foreign governments, State governments, constitutional bodies like the Union Public Service Commission, attached and subordinate offices, public enterprises, statutory authorities, public bodies, and members of the public generally.

3.2 Format

3.2.1 **Department's name and address** – Usually it is printed at the top middle of the page. In many departments, printed letter-heads are used.

3.2.2 **Number**- The letter usually bears the number of the file from which it is issued. It is written at the top middle above the department's name, although in some departments, it is written on the left side below the name of the department.

3.2.3 **Date** – It is written in numerals rather than words for the day ("18" rather than "Eighteen"). But the day may be written either after or before the month, <u>viz.</u> "June 18, 2022" or "18 June, 2022".

3.2.4 The date is usually written on the right side below the name of the department. When the number of the letter is written after the name of the department on the left side, the number and date may appear in the same line.

3.2.5 **Address -** The receiver's name and / or designation and mailing address are written on the left side. Care should be taken to show exact details, including correct spelling of the receiver's name and designation.

3.2.6 **Subject** – A brief description of the subject–matter of the letter provides focus to the receiver. It tells the receiver what the message in the letter is about, and sets the stage for the receiver to understand the message better.

3.2.7 Subject should be as specific as possible. For example, instead of saying "Ad hoc appointment", say something like "Restriction on regularization of *ad hoc* appointment".

3.2.8 **Salutation** – The standard salutation is "Sir" or "Madam", as may be appropriate. If the letter is addressed to a firm, the salutation may be "Dear Sirs".

3.2.9 **Attention line** – Occasionally, the phrase "Attention: Mr. ...." is used when it is intended to put the letter in the hands of the appropriate person.

3.2.10 **Body**– The body or text is the main message which is placed in the middle of the page. To achieve this balance, the space between the letter's parts, viz., between the letter-head, date and the receiver's address may be varied.

3.2.11 **Superscription or complimentary close** – The standard form is to close the letter with "Yours faithfully" and it is typed on the right side after the text. The name of the person who will sign the letter is written (in parenthesis) four spaces below the close. His designation and telephone number are written below the name.

3.1.12 **Enclosure**– If some document or other material is to be sent with the letter, the abbreviated word "Encl." is written on left side below the signatures, and brief description of the enclosure is given.

3.2.13 **Letter with endorsement** – Sometimes, a copy or copies of the letter may have to be sent to parties other than the one to which it is addressed. In such cases, the main letter is taken out, and on the remaining copies, the number and date of the letter is typed – number on the left side and date on the right side in the same line. The names and addresses of the parties to whom the copies are to be sent are then typed. Below these names and address, the name of the officer who will sign the endorsement, his designation, and telephone number are typed on the right side. (The name is put in parenthesis).

3.2.14 A specimen of the format of the letter is at Fig. 1, and of the letter with endorsement is at Fig. 2.

Fig. 1: SPECIMEN FORMAT OF LETTER

No.................
Government of India
(Bharat Sarkar)
Department of ....
(............... Vibhag)

New Delhi, the ...... (Date)

To

Subject

Sir,

*With reference to your letter No....................... dated................. on the subject cited above.......................

Yours faithfully,

(A.B.C.)

Under Secretary to the Govt. of India

Tele. No...............................

*Other alternative forms of the introductory phrases commonly used are:

i) In continuation of my/this Department's letter No...................

ii) With reference to the correspondence resting/ending, with your/this Department's letter No..................... dated.........................

Fig. 2: SPECIMEN FORMAT OF LETTER WITH ENDORSEMENT

No………………

Government of India
(Bharat Sarkar)
Department of …………..
(…………… Vibhag)

New Delhi, the …… (Date)

To

Subject

Sir,

*With reference to your letter No…………………… dated…………….. on the subject cited above…………………..

Yours faithfully,

(A.B.C.)
Under Secretary to the Govt. of India
Tele. No………………..

(Endorsement)

@No…………………………
@Dated…………………..

Copy forwarded for information/ necessary action to:

(1)

(2)

(A.B.C.)
Under Secretary to the Govt. of India

Tele No…………………

*Other alternative forms of the introductory phrases commonly used are:

i) In continuation of my/this Department's letter No………………..

ii) With reference to the correspondence resting/ending, with your/this Department's letter No………………… dated……………………

@To be typed on copies intended for (1) and (2) referred to in the endorsement.

4. DEMI-OFFICIAL (D.O.) LETTER

4.1 Uses– This form is generally used in correspondence between officers for an inter-change or communication of opinion or information without the formality of the prescribed procedures. It may be used when it is desired that the matter should receive personal attention of the individual addressed.

4.2 Demi-official letter is written in the first person in a personal and friendly tone. It should be addressed by an officer in a Ministry / Department who is ordinarily not more than one or two levels below the officer to whom such communication is addressed. For determining the level, Secretary / Additional Secretary are considered one level, and Director / Deputy Secretary are also considered as one level.

4.3 Communications to non-officials can also take the form of a demi-official letter, although these are not called as such.

4.4 Format

4.4.1 **Name, designation and telephone number of the sender -** These are typed on the top left side of the page.

4.4.2 **Address of the sender** - It is typed on the top right side of the page.

4.4.3 **Number** – Which is usually the file number, is typed at the top right above the address of the sender. But in some departments, it is written on the left side in the same line in which the date of the d.o. letter is written.

4.4.4 **Date -** It is typed on the right side below the address of the sender.

4.4.5 **Salutation** – The traditional salutation is "Dear Sir....." or "Dear Ms..." But if the sender is friendly with the addressee or if the addressee is at a lower level, the salutation may be "My dear.........".

4.4.6 **Subject** – It is usually not given separately, because it is mentioned in the opening sentence of the d.o. letter.

4.4.7 **Body -** The body of text is written below the solution. It is placed in the middle of the page by varying the space between the parts of the d.o. letter, viz. between the name and address of the sender and the date, and the receiver's name and address.

4.4.8 **Superscription or complimentary close -** The standard form is "Yours sincerely", which is written on the right side after the body. The name of the officer who will sign the d.o. letter is written (in parenthesis) four spaces below the close. His designation and telephone number need not be given here, as these have already been given at the top of the d.o. letter.

4.4.9 **Receiver's name, designation and address** - These are typed on the left side after one or two line spaces below signatures.

4.4.10 **Enclosure -** If any enclosure is to be sent with the d.o. letter, a notation may be made as in the case of the letter (see para 3.2.12). This notation is made on the left side below the address of the receiver.

4.4.11 A specimen of the format of a D.O. letter is at Fig. 3.

Fig. 3: SPECIMEN FORMAT OF D.O. LETTER

XYZ,

Deputy Secretary

Tele. No………………

D.O. No……………..
GOVERNMENT OF INDIA
(Bharat Sarkar)
Department of………
(……………… Vibhag)

New Delhi, the

My dear / Dear Shri

We propose to draw up a model scheme for ………………… A copy of the outline prepared in this connection is enclosed.

2. I should be grateful if you would let me have your comments as soon as possible. I may add that we intend circulating the draft scheme formally to all departments in due course for their comments.

With regards.

Yours sincerely,

(X, Y, Z)

Shri A.B.C.,

Deputy Secretary,

Department of ………………,

(…………………….. Vibhag),

KrishiBhawan, New Delhi – 110 001.

5. OFFICE MEMORANDUM (O.M.)/ MEMORANDUM/ MEMO

5.1 Uses – This form is generally used for corresponding with other departments or in calling for information from or conveying information to its employees. It may also be used in corresponding with attached and subordinate offices. It is written in the third person.

5.2 Format

5.2.1 **Department's name and address** – These are written on the top middle of the page.

5.2.2 **Number -** This is usually the file number. It is typed in the top middle above the name of the department.

5.2.3 **Date -** It is written in numerals on the right side below the name and address of the department.

5.2.4 **Title** - The title of the communication "OFFICE MEMORANDUM" is written in the middle below the date.

5.2.5 **Subject** – A brief description of the subject matter of the O.M. is given below the title.

5.2.6 **Salutation** – There is no salutation in the O.M.

5.2.7 **Body** – The body or text is typed below the subject.

5.2.8 **Superscription** – There is no superscription, except the name (in parenthesis) of the officer who will sign the O.M., and his designation and telephone number. These are written on the right side below the text.

5.2.9 **Receiver's name and address -** The name and address of the receiver is written on the left of the page after one of two line spaces below the signature. The word "To" is written on the left side above the name and address of the receiver.

5.2.10. A specimen format of O.M. is at Fig. 4.

Fig. 4: SPECIMEN FORMAT OF OFFICE MEMORANDUM

No.......................

GOVERNMENT OF INDIA

(Bharat Sarkar)

Department of ....

(.................... Vibhag)

New Delhi, the

OFFICE MEMORANDUM

Subject :

Reference is invited to this Department O.M. No... dated..............................

2. Doubts have been expressed whether the provisions of......................... also apply to.......................... It is hereby clarified that ....

(A, B, C)

Under Secretary to the Govt. of India

Tele. No...................

To
The Department of ....
(................... Vibhag)
(Shri/Smt......................................)
Yojana Bhavan,
Parliament Street,
New Delhi – 11001.

6. INTER-DEPARTMENTAL (ID) NOTE (U.O. NOTE)

6.1 **Uses -** This form is generally employed for obtaining the advice, views, concurrence, or comments of other departments on a proposal, or in seeking clarification of the existing rules, instructions etc. It may also be used by a department when consulting its attached and subordinate offices and vice versa.

6.2 **Format**

6.2.1 The inter-departmental note may either be recorded on a file referred to another department or may take the form of an independent self-contained note.

6.2.2 **Name of the department** -- The name of the department and its Branch / Section recording the note is written in the top middle of the page.

6.2.3 **Subject** – The subject need not be mentioned when the note is recorded on another department's file. But if it is an independent note, a brief description of the subject matter of the reference is given below the name of the Branch / Section recording the note.

6.2.4 **Salutation and superscription** – There is no salutation or superscription, except the name (in parenthesis), designation, and telephone number of the officer who will sign the note. These are written on the right side after the text.

6.2.5 **Body -** it is the text of the note recorded by the department concerned below the name of the department, and of the Branch / Section (when the note is recorded on the file) or below the subject (if it is an independent self- contained note).

6.2.6 **Address -** The name of the department to whom the note is being sent is written on the left side after the name and designation of the officer who will sign the note. The name and designation of the officer who should see the note are also written (in parenthesis) as a part of the address. Thereafter a line is drawn across the page, and the name of the department recording the note, the number of, note, and date are written below this line.

6.2.7 A specimen of the format of I.D. note is at Fig. 5.

Fig. 5 : SPECIMEN FORMAT OF INTER-DEPARTMENTAL NOTE

GOVERNMENT OF INDIA

(Bharat Sarkar)

Department of …………………

(………………… Vibhag)

Subject:

The present rules regulating the issue of identity cards provide *inter alia* that………..

2. A question has now arisen whether ……………………

3.

4.

5. This department will be grateful for the advice of the Department of Legal Affairs on the issue raised in para 4 above.

(X, Y, Z)

Deputy Secretary

Tele No.

Department of Legal Affairs (Vidhi KaryaVibhag), (Shri…………………………..) Shastri Bhawan, New Delhi.

Department of ………….. I.D. No………… date…………………

7. OFFICE ORDER / ORDER

7.1 Office Order – This form is normally used for issuing instructions meant for internal administration, e.g., grant of regular leave, distribution of work among officers and sections, appointments and transfers etc.

7.2 Order - This form is generally used for issuing certain types of financial sanctions and for communicating orders in disciplinary cases, etc. to the officials concerned.

7.3 Format

7.3.1 **Number -** This is usually the number of the file from which the office order / order is to be issued. It is written in the top middle of the page.

7.3.2 **Department's name -** It is written in the top middle below the number.

7.3.3 **Date -** It is shown on the right side below the department's name.

7.3.4 **Title -** The title "OFFICE ORDER", or "ORDER" is written in the middle after the date.

7.3.5 **Body** – The text of the office order or order is written below the title.

7.3.6 **Salutation and superscription** – There is no salutation or superscription, except the name (in parenthesis) and designation of the officer who will sign the office order / order. These are written on the right side below the text.

7.3.7 **Endorsement** – The names of parties to whom the copies of the office order are to be sent are listed on the left side below the name and designation of the officer signing it. The same is the case when copies of the order conveying financial sanctions are to be sent. But the order in a disciplinary case will be sent by name to the official concerned.

7.3.8 Specimens of the format of office order are at Figure 7(a) and Fig. 7(b) and of order at Fig. 8(a) and Fig. 8 (b).

Fig. 6 (a): SPECIMEN FORMAT OF OFFICE ORDER (I)

No.................
Government of India
(Bharat Sarkar)
Department of ....
(............... Vibhag)

New Delhi, the ...... (Date)

OFFICE ORDER

Shri X.Y.Z. a permanent Lower Division Clerk in this department, is granted earned leave for .... days from .... to .... with permission to prefix.......... a public holiday, to the leave.

2. It is certified that Shri X, Y, Z is likely, on the expiry of this leave, to return to duty at the station from which he proceeded on leave.

(A, B, C)

Under Secretary to the Govt. of India

Copy to :

1. Office order file
2. Cashier
3. Section concerned
4. Shri X, Y, Z
5. L.D.C.

Fig. 6 (b): SPECIMEN FORMAT OF OFFICE ORDER (II)

No..................
Government of India
(Bharat Sarkar)
Department of ....
(............... Vibhag)

New Delhi, the ...... (Date)

OFFICE ORDER

It has been decided to transfer the work relating to .... from........... Section to .... Section with immediate effect.

(A, B, C)

Under Secretary to the Govt. of India

Copy to:

Fig. 7 (a): SPECIMEN FORMAT OF ORDER (I)

No.……………….
Government of India
(Bharat Sarkar)
Department of …………..
(…………… Vibhag)

New Delhi, the …… (Date)

ORDER

Sanction of the President is accorded under rule 10 of the Delegation of Financial Powers Rules, to the write of irrecoverable loss of Rs. 5000 (Rupees Five Thousands only) being the value of the following articles belonging to this department.

(1) XXXXX

(2) XXXXXX

(A, B, C)

Under Secretary to the Govt. of India

Tel No………………….

Copy forwarded to:

1. The A.G.C.R., New Delhi.
2. Internal Finance Section
3. Cash Section

Fig. 7 (b): SPECIMEN FORMAT OF ORDER (II)

No………………
Government of India
(Bharat Sarkar)
Department of …………..
(………….. Vibhag)

New Delhi, the …… (Date)

ORDER

Shri ….………………………….., a lower division clerk in the Department of …………………………..,is hereby informed that it is proposed to take action against him under rule ………………… of …………………………..

2. Shri……………………………. is hereby given an opportunity to make such representation as he may wish to make against the proposal.

3.

4.

(D, E, F)
Under Secretary to the Govt. of India
Tel. No……………………..

To

Shri…………………….., L.D.C.

8. NOTIFICATION

8.1 Uses - This form is mostly used in notifying the promulgation of statutory rules and orders, appointments and promotions of gazetted officers, etc. through publication in the Gazette of India.

8.2 Format

8.2.1 **Publication detail -** The part and section of the gazette of India in which the notification will be published is written in parenthesis in the top middle of the page.

8.2.2 The composition of the Gazette of India and instructions for sending material for publication in the gazette are given in the Appendix.

8.2.3 **Name of the Department** – It is shown in the top middle of the page below the publication detail.

8.2.4 **Date -** It is written on the right side below the name of the department.

8.2.5 **Title** – The title "NOTIFICATION" is written in the middle below the date.

8.2.6 **Number and body -** Usually, the number of the notification is written on the left side below the title. It is followed by the text of the notification. But in the case of notification to promulgate a Statutory Order (S.O.) or a General Statutory Rule (G.S.R.), only the words "S.O." or "G.S.R." are written and the space for the number is left blank. This is filled by the press. The number of the file from which the notification is issued is given in parenthesis immediately after the text.

8.2.7 **Salutation and superscription -** There is no salutation or superscription, except the name (in parenthesis) and designation of the officer who will sign it. These are written on the right side below the text.

8.2.8 **Address -** The notification is addressed to the Manager, Government Press located at the place from where the part and the section of the gazette of India will be published (see Appendix). This address is written on the left side below the signature.

8.2.9 **Endorsement -** The number and the date are written below the address – the number on the left side and the date on the right side. Thereafter, the parties to whom the copies of the notification are to be sent are listed. The name (in parenthesis) of the officer and his designation are written on the right side below the names of the parties.

8.2.10 The endorsement is typed on all copies except the one intended for the press.

8.2.11 Specimens of the format of notification are at Fig. 8(a) and Fig. 8(b).

Fig. 8(a): SPECIMEN FORMAT OF NOTIFICATION (I)

[To be published in the Gazette of India, Part 1, Section 2]

GOVERNMENT OF INDIA
(Bharat Sarkar)
Department of ....)
(………………….. Vibhag)

New Delhi 2002

NOTIFICATION

No ………………… Shri X. Y. Z. Under Secretary in the Department of ……… is appointed to officiate as Deputy Secretary in that Department *vice* Shri………….. transferred to the Department of ………………..

(A. B. C)
Joint Secretary

To

The Manager,
Government of India Press,
(Bharat Sarkar Press) FARIDABAD

No……………………

New Delhi the Date

* Copy forwarded for information to:

(1)

(2)

(3)

(D.E.F)
Under Secretary to the Govt. of India

---

*Endorsement should be typed on all copies except the one intended for the press.

Fig.8(b): SPECIMEN FORMAT OF NOTIFICATION (2)

[To be published in the Gazette of India, Part 2, Section 3, Sub-sector (2)]

GOVERNMENT OF INDIA
(Bharat Sarkar)
Department of ……………………)
(………………….. Vibhag)

New Delhi 2002

NOTIFICATION

S.O. ………………….. In exercise of the powers conferred by Section 4 of the Supply and Prices of Goods Act, 1950 (LXX of 1950)…………………….. the Central Government hereby fix the following schedule of maximum price …………… [No……………………..]

(A, B, C)

Secretary to the Govt. of India

To
The Manager,
Government of India Press,
(Bharat Sarkar Press)
New Delhi

9. RESOLUTION

9.1 Uses - This form of communication is used for making public announcement of decisions of Government in important matters of policy, e.g., the policy of industrial licensing, appointment of committees or commissions of enquiry. Resolutions are also published in the Gazette of India.

9.2 Format

9.2.1 **Publication detail -** The part and section of the Gazette of India in which the resolution will be published is written in parenthesis in the top middle of the page.

9.2.2 **Number -** It is shown at the top middle below the publication detail.

9.2.3 **Name of the department** – It is written below the number in the middle of the page.

9.2.4 **Date -** It is written on the right side after the name of the department.

9.2.5 **Title** – The title "RESOLUTION" is written in the middle after the date.

9.2.6 **Body** – It is the text of the resolution and it is written after the title.

9.2.7 **Salutation and superscription** – There is no salutation or superscription, except the name (in parenthesis) and designation of the officer who will sign the resolution. These are written on the right side after the text.

9.2.8 **Endorsement** – After the signature, the word "ORDER" is written on the left side, and below it is "ordered" that a copy of the resolution be communicated to the parties concerned. It is "also ordered" that a copy of the resolution be published in the Gazette of India. The name (in parenthesis) and designation of the officer who will sign this endorsement is written on the right side. The address of the Manager, Government of India Press, who will publish the resolution is written on the left side after the signature.

9.2.9 A specimen of the format of resolution is at Fig. 9.

Fig. 9: SPECIMEN FORMAT OF RESOLUTION

(To be published in the Gazette of India, Part1, Section 1)

No.........................

Government of India

(Bharat Sarkar)

Department of ....

(.............. Vibhag)

New Delhi, the .... Date

RESOLUTION

The Government of India have had under consideration the question of further improving the efficiency of the departments and services concerned with the collection of revenue. As a first step in that direction the President has been pleased, under the powers vested in him by proviso to Article 309 of the Constitution of India, to decide that a Class I Central Service to be known as "Indian Revenue Service" should be constituted with effect from ....

(A, B, C)

Secretary to the Government of India

ORDER

ORDERED that a copy of the resolution be communicated to ....

ORDERED also that the resolution be published in the Gazette of India for general information.

(A, B, C)

Secretary to the Government of India

To

The Manager,
Government of India Press
(Bharat Sarkar Press)
FARIDABAD.

10. PRESS COMMUNIQUE / NOTE

10.1 Uses - This form is used when it is proposed to give wide publicity to a decision of Government. A press communiqué is more formal in character than a press note and is expected to be reproduced intact by the press. A press note, on the other hand, is intended to serve as a hand-out to the press which may edit, compress or enlarge it, as deemed fit.

10.2 Format

10.2.1 **Publication detail -** On the top of the page, instruction is given about the time and date before which the press communiqué or note is not to be published.

10.2.2 **Title** – The title "PRESS COMMUNIQUE" or "PRESS NOTE" is written in the middle after the publication detail.

10.2.3 **Body -** The text of the press communiqué or note is given below the title.

10.2.4 **Salutation or superscription -** There is no salutation or superscription in the press communiqué / note.

10.2.5 **Endorsement** – The name of the department is written in the middle below the text. The date is written on the right side after the name of the department, and the number is written on the left side. The endorsement is sent to the Principal Information Officer Press Information Bureau for issuing the communiqué / note and giving it wide publicity. The name, in parenthesis) and designation of the officer who will sign the endorsement are written on the right side after the text of the endorsement.

10.2.6 A specimen of the format of press communiqué / note is at Fig. 10.

Fig. 10: SPECIMEN FORMAT OF PRESS COMMUNIQUE / NOTE

Not to be published or broadcast before .... a.m./p.m. on.............. day the .... (Date).

PRESS COMMUNIQUE / NOTE

In response to public demand, the Government of India have appointed a Commission to go into the problem of .... and make suitable recommendations to the Government.

2. The Commission will consist of Shri........................... as Chairman and the following as members:

1.

2.

3.

3. In making its recommendations, the Commission is expected to give consideration to the following matters:

(a)

(b)

(c)

4. The Commission is expected to submit its report to the Government by ....

Department of ....

(.................... Vibhag)

New Delhi, the 2022

No..............

Forwarded to the Principal Information Officer, Press Information Bureau, Government of India, New Delhi, for issuing the communiqué / note and giving it wide publicity.

(A, B, C)

Joint Secretary

Tele. No..................

11. ENDORSEMENT

11.1 Uses – As an independent form of communication, endorsement is used when a paper has to be retuned in original to the sender, or the paper in original or its copy is to be sent to another department or office for information or action. Another form of endorsement is when a copy of a communication is proposed to be forwarded to parties other than the one to which the main communication is addressed, such as in the case of letter or a notification. Normally, this form will not be used in sending copies to State Governments. The appropriate form for such communication should be a letter.

11.2 Format

11.2.1 The format of endorsement when used as an independent form of communication is described in the following paragraphs.

11.2.2 **Number -** The number is written at the top middle of the page.

11.2.3 **Name of the department** – It is written at the top middle below the number.

11.2.4 **Date** – It is shown on the right side after the name of the department.

11.2.5 **Body** – It is the text that is written after the date. The standard text is "A copy of the under-mentioned papers is forwarded to …………… for information and necessary action". The name of the party to whom the endorsement is to be sent is written in the blank space. Thus the addressee is also mentioned in the text itself.

11.2.6 **Salutation and superscription** – There is no salutation and superscription, except the name (in parenthesis), designation, and telephone number of the officer who will sign the endorsement.

11.2.7 **Details of papers forwarded** – A list of papers which are to be forwarded is given on the left side after signatures. This list is given after writing the words "List of papers forwarded".

11.2.8 A specimen of the format of endorsement as an independent communication is at Fig. 11.

Fig. 11: SPECIMEN FORMAT OF ENDORSEMENT

No.......................
Government of India
(Bharat Sarkar)
Department of ....
(.............. Vibhag)

New Delhi, the ...... (Date)

ENDORSEMENT

A copy each of the under-mentioned papers is forwarded to...................... for information and necessary action.

(A, B, C)

Secretary to the Government of India

Tele No.................

List of papers forwarded:

(1)

(2)

(3)

NOTE: The above is a specimen of endorsement as an independent form of communication. There can, however, be endorsement below other forms of communication also, e.g., letter or notification, as shown in specimen at Fig. 2 and Fig. 9 (a).

12. CIRCULAR

12.1 Uses – This form is used when important and urgent external communications received or important and urgent decisions taken internally have to be circulated within a department for information and compliance by a large number of employees.

12.2 Format - The format of circular is similar to that of endorsement, except that the title "CIRCULAR" is written in the middle of the page after the date.

13. E-MAIL

13.1 Uses:E-mail a paperless form of communication which departments having computer facilities supported by internet or internet connectivity use. It is being widely used for subjects where legal or financial implications are not involved. The email services provided by NIC shall be used for official communication by Departments in e-office environment. It can be widely used even where classified data is shared. Such classified data are to be sent only in encrypted version. Other guidelines are provided in the 'E-mail Policy of Government of India'.

Computer has changed the entire gamut of human life at an overwhelming pace. It is an electronic equipment which is capable of creating solutions by performing complex processing of information without manual intervention and that too at tremendous speed.

13.1.1 The principles for communicating electronically are pretty the same as for communication on paper, although the trend is towards brevity. If we do not know how to write and how to send and receive these, we are treated as illiterates. Here, we shall discuss main features of e-mail.

13.1.2 As use of computer in the workplace has become increasingly more common, so has the usage of communicating via electronic mail, known more familiarly as "e-mail." Electronic communications may seem ephemeral, but they are most definitely not! E-mails, in particular, are eternal. As soon as we have sent one, we have instantly created four copies: one on our own PC, one on our server, one on recipient's sever and one on our recipient's PC. Automatic back-ups create more copies. A year after sending a message, there could be 50 or more copies. There is practically no way of ensuring that one of these copies won't survive and be forwarded to or read by others, on purpose or inadvertently. E-mails can even be used as evidence in court.

13.1.3 If what you say is negative or could be taken wrongly, consider deleting it, or rewording it. If it must be said, consider using the telephone or meeting face to face to deliver your message instead. Don't E-mail it.

13.1.4 As with any written communication, we can never be sure who will see it. With E-mails in particular, then, you should write assuming that others will read it. A good rule of thumb is: don't write anything you wouldn't want your employer or your family to read.

13.1.5 If you're e-mailing on your employer's equipment, the e-mail is their property and they have the right to intercept it and read it. They are also legally responsible for the contents, so watch what you E-mail

13.2 WATCH YOUR TONE

13.2.1 The impersonal and speedy nature of electronic communications can make us seem unintentionally rude if we're not careful. Without body language or voice tone cues to help recipients gauge the strength of our message or our feelings, they're likely to take the most negative spin possible. Short sentences, lack of salutations, a desire to be brief, can all make our electronic communications seem overly curt. A brief and direct message can come across as terse; humour can fall flat; and mild frustration or annoyance can translate into rage.

13.2.2 To make sure this doesn't happen to you, try to picture how the receiver will react to your message. Have you inadvertently been sarcastic, condescending, demanding or judgmental? Never fire off a fax or e-mail in anger. If you feel you must write the message, do so, but don't send it for at least 24 hours. You may have cooled off by then.

13.2.3 Take extra care to be tactful and to set a friendly and courteous tone. Remember your usual Ps and Qs—please and thank you.

13.3 GENERAL GUIDELINES

13.3.1 Among the general guidelines that apply to the drafting and sending of e-mails is the advice not to key the text of a message in all uppercase (CAPITAL) letters, which is the equivalent of yelling at the recipient. "Cute" little symbolic messages made from punctuation marks called emoticons (such as ☺ for a 'smiley face') and acronyms (such as BCNU for, be seeing you', BTW for 'by the way') are probably best avoided since not everyone knows about them, or likes them. Another advisable practice is to be concise, remembering that many professionals receive a multitude of e-mails throughout the day and often don't have the time to read thoroughly each piece of correspondence. Because the recipient may have to evaluate which incoming messages have the greatest priority, it may be to the sender's advantage to use the subject line as an attention grabber, especially if the objective is to get a response as soon as possible. Also, the subject line can be used to identify the sender, as sometimes the reading of e-mail may be delayed because the recipient does not recognize the sender's name or address. If the sender is unknown, or the subject-line message is particularly obscure or cryptic, there is a chance that the recipient may, as a precautionary measure against viruses, disregard the e-mail altogether and delete the message without opening it.

13.3.2 E-mail messages being sent off-site should end with a closing signature that includes the sender's full name and organization affiliation. Most e-mail programmes provide an option whereby a closing signature may be created and automatically appended to all outgoing messages.

13.3.3 It is good practice to use the "reply" option to an existing message rather than opening a "new message" page. The "reply" gives the recipient a link, commonly called a thread, to the original message, and a path to follow if several replies to one message pile up. Or, if the incoming message is lengthy and only certain items require a response, the sender can copy only those relevant parts and paste them into a "new message," then key in the appropriate responses. A standard technique (often performed automatically by e-mail software) for indicating which text was excerpted from the original is to precede that text with a greater-than symbol (>). For example:

> Will you be available for a meeting on Tuesday, March 19? [from the original incoming message]

Yes, that's fine, [response]

13.4 E-MAIL DOS:

13.4.1 In the Government and in the public sector undertakings, the officials MUST only use official E-mail accounts created by the National Informatics Centre (NIC) and not private popular ones like gmail.com or hotmail.com accounts for security reasons. The National Informatics Centre's E-mail server (Network Computer) makes it mandatory to have passwords with special characters (%, and, # etc.), one numeric and one capital letter. A password typed on the home page is stored and sent to NIC servers in encrypted form. NIC's spam guard does not allow .rar and .ext files to be sent to a user's inbox.

13.4.2 *Be sure that the people with whom you plan to communicate are comfortable receiving e-mail.* Not everyone is.

13.4.3 *Consider your readers.* Ask yourself how they might react to what you've written.

13.4.4 *Provide a clear, specific subject line.* Be sure it's meaningful at a glance. If the recipient has an in-box replete with messages (some people receive more than 100 a day), he or she will decide which to read based on the relative importance of senders and subjects. Users often respond to the volume of their e-mail by using filters and rules-based agents. If your message has been filed, the recipient can find it quickly by checking the subject area.

13.4.5 *Use excerpts from previous messages to clarify what you're replying to.* To distinguish the earlier text from your current responses, insert the ">" symbol in front of the quoted material and follow it with your response. This example shows how such a text will look on your screen:

> How about 3:00 p.m. on Thursday for the meeting?

That will work for me.

> Can we count on a report from you concerning your group's progress?

Yes. It'll take about five minutes.

This technique is preferable to quoting an entire message and adding "OK," "Me, too," or "I agree."

13.4.6 *Remove long lists of recipients' names and addresses.* These require the recipient to scroll down in order to get to your message, and some of your correspondents might not like having their e-mail addresses made available to other people. Use the BCC ("blind carbon copy") feature to suppress the names of other recipients.

13.4.7 *Strike a balance between formal and casual language.* Your message creates an image of your organization and you. When communicating with upper management or customers, use a business letter format, complete sentences, and a spell-checker. Misspelled or omitted words indicate a lack of attention to detail. If you're just trying to set up a meeting with your colleague in the next cubicle, casual language is appropriate.

13.4.8 *Read and then reread your message before you send it.* Be sure that your message is clear and grammatically correct. Attention to detail is as important in e-mail as it is in other forms of written communication. Double-check the spelling of recipients' addresses. A missed keystroke will result in undelivered mail. After sending e-mail, check back in case you've received an "undeliverable" error message. Save a sender's address to your address book, which allows you to avoid retyping the address and introducing errors.

13.4.9 *Key in your name at the end of your message.* It identifies you as the sender, and its common courtesy.

13.4.10 *Be careful how you present your message.* Double-check your formatting. Your message may look quite different on your recipient's screen than it does on yours. Avoid fancy fonts and the use of special characters which may result in a garbled message.

13.4.11 *Acknowledge receipt of messages promptly.* If you're going to be out of the office, use auto-response messages.

13.4.12 *Observe the common practices of your organization.* Every organization has its own "culture." If you're not familiar with a new system, ask someone who is familiar before sending messages.

13.5 E-MAIL DON'TS:

Most of these rules are practices that are inappropriate in any form of businesscommunication because they are either rude or unprofessional. With so many new (and inexperienced) e-mail users going online every day, the rules need to be made explicit.

13.5.1 *Never substitute e-mail for necessary face-to-face meetings,* especially when praising work well done, reprimanding someone, or firing someone. Such communications should be handled in person.

13.5.2 *Never assume that e-mail is private.* Something can go wrong with any software programme, and your e-mail might be misdirected. Also, many organizations monitor their employees' e-mail. Don't send anything via e-mail that you wouldn't post to the organization bulletin board. If your message is personal, ask for a face-to-face meeting or send it via regular mail.

13.5.3 *Don't assume that everyone reads e-mail immediately.* E-mail travels quickly, but speed of transmission does not guarantee speed of communication. Some people don't check their e-mail in-box every day. Others may set aside a particular time of the day to check their e-mail, but respond only to messages that require immediate attention. Sometimes days or weeks can pass between when a message is sent and when it is read. If you need an immediate response, put "urgent" or "please read immediately" in the subject line, preceding the specific subject of the message.

13.5.4 *Never send an angry message via e-mail.* There's no time in business when such correspondence is appropriate.

13.5.5 *Never send an e-mail message written in capital letters, LIKE THIS!* Using all capital letters in any context is regarded as the e-mail equivalent of shouting.

13.5.6 *Never forward jokes, spam, chain letters, or advertisements.* They will annoy colleagues and potential customers.

13.5.7 *Do not reply to everyone who received an e-mail unless it's relevant to them.* If you're simply acknowledging receipt or confirming the time of a meeting, respond only to the sender.

13.5.8 *Do not send anyone a large attached file unless the person is expecting it.* If a document is really important, send it by overnight delivery.

13.5.9 *Do not send files in HTML unless it's requested.* Some servers cannot handle messages in HTML, and your message will arrive garbled. Such documents can actually cause the recipient's software programme to crash.

13.5.10 *Do not use e-mail for any illegal or unethical purpose.* This should go without saying.

13.6 THE BIGGEST E-MAIL MISTAKES

E-mail is a great tool but can sometimes be a bit perilous. Sloppiness and carelessness can not only get you in trouble, they can lead to your organization's e-mail system crashing. Anyone who uses e-mail should avoid the following mistakes:

13.6.1 Giving *confidential information in an e-mail.* Your credit card number, for instance, can easily be sent throughout in the world.

13.6.2 *Opening attachments from strangers.* Never open an e-mail that has an attachment that is vague or says "Check this out!" A virus may spread by invading the contact list on a computer and sending itself to every e-mail address on the list.

13.6.3 *Opening unsolicited e-mail without first scanning for viruses.* There are several free anti-virus programmes available. Check with your organization's IT or MIS department to see what they recommend.

13.6.4 *Hitting "reply" to an unsolicited e-mail when asking to be taken off the sender's list.* By hitting "reply" you may be opening up your account to a deluge of spam.

13.6.5 *Hitting "reply all" when only the sender needs a response.* If you receive an e-mail from someone in the organization who asks for feedback on an issue, remember to hit "reply."

13.6.6 *Sending "all@" e-mails.* Being able to send e-mail to everyone in your organization at once is not a right. Very few organizations in the world allow employees the right to send e-mails to the entire organization without some approval process. So remember, just because you are desperate to sell your idea, that doesn't mean the CEO needs an e-mail about it.

13.6.7 *Sending an e-mail without a signature.* Your business e-mail should have a preset signature at the bottom. Make sure you use organization colours and logos if provided. Never use a virtual business card attachment (unless it is an organization protocol). It may be mistaken for a virus.

13.6.8 *Sending an e-mail without spell-checking it.* E-mail is official correspondence. Most e-mail systems spell-check as you type or have a "spell-check before sending" setting.

13.6.9 *Sending e-mail without a "subject" line or sending e-mail with a vague subject line.* Be specific. A subject that reads "Lastest Info on Johnson Account" will get more attention than one that reads "FYI" or "new data." A blank subject line may get no attention at all.

13.7 Understanding and mastering writing E-mails and how to send and receive these would help us further improve our communication skills. One should follow the guidelines, do's and don'ts discussed here scrupulously. One should keep track of further advances, master them and thus update their knowledge and skill in communicating electronically

14. CONCLUSION

14.1 Written communication is an important means of conveying and receiving information and reaching important decisions. Effective communication will require good writing skills. Good writing skills are, therefore, in demand everywhere. Equally important is the form one adopts for one's writing. In Government departments the forms of written communication have been developed to cater to the multifarious needs of Government functioning. A proper understanding of these forms will add to the efficient and effective functioning of Government departments.

Appendix

COMPOSITION OF THE GAZETTE OF INDIA AND INSTRUCTIONS FOR SENDING MATERIAL FOR PUBLICATION THEREIN.

A. COMPOSITION

Part	Section	Type of matter to be published
I. To be published from Faridabad.	1	Notifications relating to resolutions and non-statutory orders issued by the Ministries of the Government of India (other than the Ministry of Defence).
	2	Notifications regarding appointments, promotions etc. of Government Officers issued by the Ministries of the Government of India (other than the Ministry of Defence)
	3	Notifications relating to resolutions and non-statutory orders issued by the Ministry of Defence.
	4	Notifications regarding appointments, promotions, etc. of Government Officers issued by the Ministry of Defence.
II. To be published from Delhi	1	Acts, ordinances and regulations.
	1A	Publication of the authoritative texts in Hindi language of Acts, ordinances and regulations.
	2	Bills and reports of Select Committees on Bills.
	3	*Sub-Section (i)* General statutory rules (including orders, byelaws, etc., of a general character) issued by the Ministries of the Government of India (other than the Ministry of Defence) and by Central authorities (other than the administrations of UnionTerritories). *Sub-Section (ii)* Statutory orders and notifications issued by the Ministries of the Government of

		India (other than the Ministry of Defence) and by Central authorities (other than the administrations of UnionTerritories).
	3A	Authoritative texts in Hindi (other than such texts published in section 3 or section 4) of general statutory rules and statutory orders (including bye-laws of general character) issued by the Ministries of the Government of India (including the Ministry of Defence) and by Central authorities (other than administrations of UnionTerritories).
	4	Statutory rules and orders issued by the Ministry of Defence.
III. To be published from Faridabad.	1	Notifications issued by the Supreme Court. Comptroller and Auditor General, Union Public Service Commission, Railway Administration, High Courts and the attached and subordinates offices of the Government of India.
	2	Notifications and notices issued by the Patent Office, Kolkata.
	3	Notifications issued by or under the authority of Chief Commissioners/Administrators of UnionTerritories.
	4	Miscellaneous notifications including notifications, orders, advertisements and notices issued by the statutory bodies.
IV. To be published from Faridabad		Advertisements and notices by private individuals and private bodies.
V. To be published from Faridabad		Supplement showing statistics of births and deaths, etc. both in English and Hindi.

NOTE 1 – Notifications to be published in sub-section (i) of Section 3 of Part II are serial numbered by press as 'G.S.R.................... and those published in sub-

section (ii) as S.O................. The identification numbers given by the Ministries will appear within brackets at the end of notification.

NOTE 2 – Weekly statement of the Reserve Bank of India published by the Central Government under Section 53(i) of the Reserve Bank of India Act, 1934 is published in sub-section (ii) of Section 3 of Part II.

NOTE 3 - Part II of the Gazette is published in octavo form so that each section might be bound at the end of the year in a form convenient for reference.

B. INSTRUCTIONS

1. The part and the section of the gazette in which the matter is to be published (vide 'A instructions' above) should invariably be indicated on the top of the copy for the guidance of the press. In case of doubt as to whether a notification should be treated as a statutory rule or order and published in sub-section (i) or sub-section (ii) of Section 3, as the case may be, of Part II, the Ministry of Law should be consulted.

2. The original type-script copy, signed by a competent officer, should alone be sent to the press. Cyclostyled copy, carbon copy or a copy which does not bear the officer's signature will not be accepted by the press. Corrections, if any, in the copy sent to the press, should be legible and attested by the officer signing it.

3. Extraordinary issues of the Gazette can be published whenever necessary. No matter should be required to be published in a Gazette Extraordinary unless it is of such urgent nature that it cannot wait until the publication of the next ordinary issue of the Gazette.

4. In fixing the date which a Gazette Extraordinary should bear, the time-schedule prescribed by the Chief Controller of Printing and Stationery should be observed. Where for any special reasons this is not practicable, the Government Press should be consulted before fixing a date.

5. The notification to be published in a Gazette Extraordinary or the forwarding letter should invariably be signed by an officer not lower in rank than a joint secretary.

6. All notifications intended for publication as 'extraordinary issues' irrespective of the part, section, or sub-section, in which they are to appear, should be sent to the Government of India Press, New Delhi. The part and the section of the Gazette in which the notification would normally have been published will be indicated by that press in the issue itself.

7. 15 copies of every notification of general public importance will be sent by the department issuing it to the Parliament Library at the same time when it is sent for publication in the Gazette of India. A copy of the letter, forwarding the copies to the Parliament Library, will be endorsed to the Lok Sabha Secretariat and the Rajya Sabha Secretariat along with a copy of concerned Notification to each of them.

8. Not less than ten copies of every statutory Notification will be sent by the department issuing it to the Legislative Department of the Ministry of Law on the date on which it is sent for publication in the Gazette of India.

9. Copy of every Gazette Notification will be sent by the Organization issuing it to all the concerned Ministries / Departments at the same time when it is sent for publication in the Gazette of India.

EXERCISES

EXERCISE – 1

Fill in the blank in each of the following sentences by picking up the option, which you consider to be correct, from among those given below each sentence.

1. Letter is a principal form of communication with …………………

   a) the employees within the organisation.
   b) other departments of the government.
   c) officers in other departments to draw attention to delayed cases.
   d) members of the public generally.

2. Office memorandum is generally used for corresponding with ……………

   a) constitutional bodies like the Union Public Service Commission.
   b) heads of public enterprises.
   c) other departments of Government.
   d) State Government.

3. An office order is …………………………

   a) generally issued conveying financial sanctions.
   b) a usual form for communicating orders in disciplinary cases.
   c) normally used for issuing instructions meant for internal administration.
   d) frequently used for drawing attention of outstation parties on matters demanding prompt attention.

4. Notification is a form mostly used for notifying ………………

   a) appointments and promotions of gazetted officers.
   b) orders about grant of leave and distribution of work among employees.
   c) decisions of Government in disciplinary cases.
   d) decisions of Government for giving wide publicity.

EXERCISE – 2

Fill in the blank in each of the following sentences by picking up the option, which you consider to be correct, from among those given below each sentence.

1. In a letter, mention of "Subject"......................................
   a) is unnecessary, as it can be written in the text of the letter.
   b) distracts the reader from the message in the letter.
   c) takes away the surprise element in the message.
   d) tells the receiver what the message in the letter is about.

2. In a D.O. letter, the name, designation and telephone number of the sender is written ....
   a) on the top left side of the page.
   b) at the bottom of the page.
   c) on the top right side of the page.
   d) immediately below the signatures.

3. In an office order ....
   a) there is no superscription, but the standard salutation "Sir" or "Madam" is always written.
   b) the title "OFFICE ORDER" is written in the middle after the date.
   c) the date is shown on the left side immediately after the name of the department.
   d) the endorsement should merely show that copies be sent "to all concerned".

4. Press communiqué ....
   a) is the same as a press note and there is no difference between the two in the manner these are used.
   b) begins with the standard salutation 'Sir' or 'Madam'.
   c) is more formal than a press note.
   d) can be published on the date and time as the Press Information Officer may decide.

EXERCISE – 3

Fill in the blank in each of the following sentences by picking up the option, which you consider to be correct, from among those given below each sentence.

1. In a d.o. letter, the standard form of superscription is ....

   a) "Sincerely yours"
   b) "Yours sincerely"
   c) "Your truly"
   d) "Your best friend"

2. In an office memorandum.................

   a) the number is usually given at the end of the text.
   b) it is unnecessary to give the title "Office Memorandum".
   c) the subject is not written separately because it is written as a part of the text.
   d) there is no salutation or superscription, except the name, designation, and telephone number of the officer who will sign it.

3. In an office order,.....................

   a) the names of parties to whom copies of the office order are to be sent are listed on the left side below the name and designation of the officer who will sign it.
   b) it is a matter of courtesy to write the superscription "Yours faithfully" above the name and designation of the officer who will sign it.
   c) it is customary for the officer who signs the main copy, to sign all endorsements also.
   d) the parties to whom copies are to be endorsed are listed at the top of the office order.

4. In a press communiqué.........

   a) on the top of the page, instruction is given about the time and date before which it should not be published.
   b) the title "PRESS COMMUNIQUE" is written at the bottom after the text.
   c) in the endorsement, the name of the department is written below the designation of the officer who will sign the communiqué.
   d) it is customary to use the salutation "Dear Sir's", before the text.

EXERCISE 4

Fill in the blank in each of the following sentences by picking up the option, which you consider to be correct, from among those given below each sentence.

1. In a letter, the standard form of superscription is................

   a) "Your obedient servant".
   b) "Yours faithfully".
   c) "Yours sincerely".
   d) "Yours truly".

2. In a D.O. letter, the name, designation, and address of the receiver are given.............

   a) on the top of the page below the name, designation and address of the sender.
   b) at the bottom right side of the page.
   c) on the left side after one or two line spaces below signatures.
   d) on the right side immediately below signatures.

3. In an office order.................

   a) the department's name is written only as a part of the name and designation of the officer who will sign the office order.
   b) the number, which is usually the file number, is written in the top middle of the page.
   c) the date is written at the bottom left side after the text.
   d) the title "Office Order" is written in the top right side of the page.

4. In a press note,..................

   a) the title "PRESS NOTE" is written below the text of the note.
   b) both salutation "Sir" or "Madam", and superscription "Yours faithfully" are used as a matter of courtesy.
   c) the endorsement is sent to the Principal Information Officer for issuing the note and giving it wide publicity.
   d) in the endorsement, the number is written on the right side and date on the left side after the name of the department.

EXERCISE 5

Fill in the blank in each of the following sentences by picking up the option, which you consider to be correct, from among those given below each sentence.

1. In a letter with endorsement ....
   a) the main letter is taken out and on the remaining copies the names and addresses of parties to whom the endorsement is to be sent are typed.
   b) endorsement is typed on all copies, including the main letter.
   c) separate endorsement is typed for each party, and names and addresses of other parties do not appear at the endorsement.
   d) it is not necessary for anyone to sign the endorsement.
2. In an office memorandum (O.M.) ....
   a) the name and address of the receiver is written on the left of the page after one or two lines space below the signatures.
   b) the name and address of the receiver is given at the top right side of the page after date.
   c) the standard salutation "Sir" or "Madam" is given on the left of the page after the subject.
   d) the body or text is written after the names of both the issuing department and the receiving department have been written side by side.
3. Office order and order...................
   a) are similar for all purposes and these terms can be used interchangeably in all cases of internal administration and financial sanctions.
   b) have different forms to show the number in on office order, the number is always given at the end after the text, whereas in an order, it is given immediately before the text.
   c) both have different uses – 'office order' for internal administration, and 'order' for financial sanctions or for conveying decisions in disciplinary cases.
   d) both reflect authoritative style of functioning and are meant to suppress employees.
4. In a resolution.................
   a) the part and section of the Gazette of India in which it will be published is written in the top middle of the page.
   b) the name of the department is written below the number at the top left of the page.
   c) there is no superscription but the salutation "Dear Sir" or "Dear Madam", as may be appropriate, should always be used.
   d) it is not necessary to give any title as its form already shows that it is a resolution.

EXERCISE – 6

Tick mark (✓) under the heading 'True' or 'False'.

S.No.	Statements	True	False
1.	E-mail is private. It can be opened only by you.		
2.	You can always forward jokes, spam, chain letters or advertisements through E-mail. Your colleagues and potential customers will welcome these.		
3.	You should not send 'all@' E-mails in your organization.		
4.	Don't assume that every one reads E-mail immediately.		
5.	You can always send an angry message via E-mail.		
6.	Do not send files in HTML unless the person is expecting these so.		
7.	Remove long list of recipients' names and addresses. Use the BCC ("Blind carbon copy") feature to suppress the names of other recipients of E-mail.		
8.	The National Informatics Centre's E-mail server (Network Computer) makes it mandatory to have passwords with special characters (%, and, # etc.) , one numeric and one capital letter		
9.	It is good practice to use the "reply" option to an existing message rather than opening a "new message" page.		
10.	In e-file, the issue can be made electronically through emails and an office copy of the issue gets automatically attached to the file along with any enclosures sent.		
11.	KMS allowusers to create and managee-documents which can be viewed, searched and shared. It is also capable of keeping track of the different versions modified by different users.		
12	Dealing Hand is not responsible for retaining office copy of the communication such as emails sent, including attachment(s) or downloading and filing it in appropriate folders in e-Office system.		

ANSWERS

EXERCISE - 1

1. (d)   2. (c)   3. (c)   4. (a)

EXERCISE - 2

1. (d)   2. (a)   3. (b)   4. (c)

EXERCISE - 3

1. (b)   2. (d)   3. (a)   4. (a)

EXERCISE - 4

1. (b)   2. (c)   3. (b)   4. (c)

EXERCISE - 5

1. (a)   2. (a)   3. (c)   4. (a)

EXERCISE – 6

1. (False)   2. (True)   3. (True)   4. (True)   5. (False)

6. (True)   7. (True)   8. (True)   9. (True)   10. (True)

11. (True)   12. (False)

Chapter - Six

NOTING

1. INTRODUCTION

1.1 Senior officers in the government, while dealing with cases generally depend on the views of their Office Assistants (dealing hands) expressed through 'notes' on files. A 'note' is remarks recorded on a case. 'Noting' is the process of recording a 'note' on the noting portion of a file. 'Note' is recorded by dealing hands or other officers in the hierarchy to facilitate decision making by competent authorities. The note helps the officer in understanding the case and therein early disposal of the case.

1.2 The Note may be in any of the following forms:

(i) Brief remarks on a simple or routine case;

(ii) A precis of previous papers, in a case in which exchange of views, through notes and / or correspondence, have been for a long period of time, and it is necessary to give an overview of the whole case so that a decision may be made;

(iii) A statement of the case in which views of the parties consulted have been obtained and a decision is now required;

(iv) An analysis of questions requiring decision in a complicated case which has been examined in detail;

(v) Views, comments, and suggestions made by the persons who have considered the case at different levels. These may include suggestions about alternative courses of actions, the implications of each such course, and recommendation about the most appropriate course of action; and

(vi) Final orders passed in the case.

2. CASES WHERE NOTING IS NOT REQUIRED

2.1 Noting is not required when, in a case, the line of action is obvious, or is based on a clear precedent or practice, or has been indicated by a higher officer, and a communication is to be sent. In such matters, a fair copy of the communication or a draft, or a draft with fair copy of the communication, as case may be can be put up.

2.2 Noting may not be necessary when dealing with cases of repetitive nature, such as sanctioning of leave, GPF advances, forwarding of applications, and the like. In such cases, Standard Process Sheets should be devised with the approval of the Branch Officer. A Standard Process Sheet is a skeleton note developed for repetitive items of work. It shows pre-determined points of check or aspects to be noted upon, and also has space for the sanctioning or approving authority to pass his orders. By filling blanks in these sheets, answers of check points are given and the competent authority can give his orders on the basis of these answers.

3. CASES WHERE NOTING IS REQUIRED

3.1 Noting is necessary in cases which required examination or in which an officer has given directions for its examination.

3.2 Noting will also be necessary when the office initiates a proposal on its own for consideration and approval.

4. ACTION BEFORE NOTING IN A CASE

4.1 Before writing a note the dealing hand should check that all statements made in the receipt, insofar as they are open to check, are correct, and that there are no mistakes or misstatement of facts. If there are any such discrepancy, this should first be reconciled. In such a case, a brief note pointing out the discrepancy may be put up for approval of higher officers. Further action on the receipt may be taken after the discrepancy has been reconciled.

5. WHAT TO WRITE IN A NOTE?

5.1 When writing a note, the following points should be covered, wherever applicable:

(i) Draw attention, where necessary, to legal position or precedents or conventions and point out the relevant law and rules. Copies of such law, rules, and precedents should also be put up.

(ii) Furnish any other relevant data or information available in the office for fuller understanding of the case.

(iii) State the questions for consideration and bring out clearly the points requiring decision.

(iv) Suggest, where possible, alternative courses of action, and indicate the implications of each one of them.

(v) Suggest the most appropriate course of action and give its justification.

(vi) If acceptance of the suggestion will involve expenditure of money, the position about the availability of funds, and, where necessary, views of the finance department or finance branch, if consulted, should also be stated.

(vii) Indicate the authority whose approval or sanction is required in the case.

6. PRINCIPLES OF EFFECTIVE NOTE WRITING

A note is a piece of writing intended for internal use within the organization. Therefore, the principles of effective writing should be followed in writing notes. Thus, a note should be.

(i) **Complete**, i.e., it should answer all questions that have been raised and all other possible questions that may arise while considering the case. Answers to questions such as **What**, **Why**, **How**, **When**, **Where**, and **Who** will help in making the note complete.

(ii) **Clear**, i.e., it should be written, as far as possible, choosing short, familiar words, using short sentences, in active voice, and preferring concrete expressions in place of abstract ones.

(iii) **Concise and to the point**, i.e., it should not contain wordy expressions, or trite or unnecessary expressions, and should include only relevant statements. It should also avoid repetitions either of words or ideas.

(iv) **Coherent**, i.e., it should be logically arranged, sticking to one idea for each paragraph, and linking together sentences and paragraphs.

(v) **Correct**, i.e., it should be factually correct, figures should be free from mistakes, and the writing should be grammatically correct.

(vi) **Courteous**, i.e., it should express ideas tactfully, without hurting anybody's feelings, and emphasise positive facts. If apparent errors or incorrect statements in a case have to be pointed out or if an opinion expressed therein has to be criticized, care should be taken to couch the observations in courteous and temperate language free from personal remarks.

(vii) Organised properly, i.e., it should put ideas in the best order for impact, reflecting clear thinking. The first paragraph should state the main point followed by paragraphs giving evidence and discussing it, and the final paragraph should contain recommendations.

(viii) Visually attractive, i.e., it should be made attractive by dividing the note in serially numbered paragraphs, using headings liberally, and keeping the paragraphs of six to ten lines each. Where possible use bullets and other lists, and leave a small margin of about one inch on all sides (left, right, top and bottom).

7. GUIDELINES FOR WRITING NOTES:

(i) Notes and orders should normally be recorded on note sheets (green sheets) in the note portion of the file.

(ii) A note is submitted either to seek approval of the competent authority or for information.

(iii) Notes should be typed or written on both sides of the note sheet.

(iv) Black or blue ink should be used by all category of staff and officers. Only an officer of the level of Joint Secretary of Government of India and above may use green or red ink in rare cases.

(v) A note must be concise and to the point. Lengthy notes are to be avoided. The verbatim reproduction of extracts from or paraphrasing of the paper under consideration, fresh receipt, or any other part of correspondence or notes on the same file, should not be attempted. Instead, a summarized version of the issues raised in PUC/FR are to be brought on the note.

(vi) When passing orders or making suggestions, an officer should confine his note to the actual points he proposes to make without reiterating the ground already covered in previous notes. If he agrees to the line of action suggested in the preceding note, he should merely append his signature. In case he takes a decision different from the one on the file, he may do so giving reasons for his decision.

(vii) Any officer, who has to note upon a file on which a running summary of facts is available should, in drawing attention to the facts of the case, refer to the appropriate part of the summary without repeating it in his own note.

(viii) Relevant extracts or a rule or instruction should be placed on the file and attention to it should be drawn in the note, rather than reproducing the relevant provisions in the note unless such an extract on the note is necessary to arrive at a decision.

(ix) Unless a running summary of facts is already available on the file or the last note on the file itself serves that purpose, a self-contained note should be put up with every case submitted to the highest authority of the organization. Such a note should bring out briefly but clearly relevant facts, including the views expressed on the subject by other departments, if any, consulted in the matter and the point or points on which the orders of the highest authority are sought.

(x) A self-contained note is prepared while seeking advice or opinion or concurrence of other Departments with prior permission by authorized officer.

(xi) When a paper under consideration raises several major points which require detailed examination and respective orders, each point (or group of related points) should be noted upon separately in section notes; such notes should each begin with a list of the major point(s) dealt with therein and placed below the main note in a separate folder.

(xii) If apparent errors or incorrect statements in a case have to be pointed out or if an opinion expressed therein has to be countered, care should be taken to make observations in courteous and temperate language free from personal remarks.

(xiii) A small margin of about an inch should be left on all sides (left, right, top and bottom) of each page of the note sheet to ensure better preservation of notes recorded on the files as at times the paper gets torn from the edges making reading of the document difficult.

(xiv) A note should be divided into serially numbered paragraphs briefly titled.

(xv) The dealing hand should append his full signature with date on the left below his note. An officer should append his full signature on the right hand side of the note with name, designation, and date.

(xvi) If the note has been written till the end of the page, and there is no blank sheet thereafter, a blank note sheet should be added to the file, so that the officer is not inconvenienced in writing his note or giving his orders.

E-file

Creation of electronic file (e-file)

1. *In e-file, electronic file or physical file (a file on which file number is created by the system but processing on the file is done physically) is created before recording a note, using appropriate menu option.*

2. *No classified information shall be handled through e-office as per extant policy in force. E-office is only for processing of unclassified information. It is re-iterated that classified documents (secret and top secret), shall strictly be carried out only in a standalone computer or connected on a dedicated network air gaped from internet.*

Recording a note in an electronic file

The inner page of e-file has "Add Green Note" option to record the note, and do the referencing, docketing, etc. "Yellow Note" option is selected to prepare a rough note, which may then be confirmed as a Green Note. Details of name etc. of the officer who confirms it will appear in Green note.

The officers may be provided Virtual Private Network (VPN) for working in e-office from home in non-classified e-files only. Issue of VPNs should be with due diligence and security aspects should be reviewed from time to time. Additional security features may be got introduced if necessary for secure use of VPN.

All officers of the rank of Dealing officers and above or equivalent to use Digital Signature Certificates (DSC) or e-sign for electronically signing the e-files in e-Office system.

DSC are to be procured by individual organisations. For using the e-sign, it is required that individual's mobile number is linked to his/her Aadhar Number.

There are provisions for standardized one-line quick noting.

e-file has the facility of delegating access of e-file of a user to another user with complete or restricted rights. There are different kinds of delegation as follows-

S. No.	*Signatory Delegation*	*Secretarial Assistance*	*Authority Delegation*
1.	*User to whom charge is delegated have to login using his/her own e-Office account and DSC token*	*User to whom charge is delegated have to login using his/her own e-Office account and DSC token*	*User to whom charge is delegated have to login using his/her own e-Office account and DSC token*
2.	*User has the Read/Write/Send rights of files belonging to the delegated account.*	*User has the Read (for both physical and electronic) / Write (for both physical and electronic) / Send (only for physical) rights of the files belonging to the delegated account.*	*User has the Read/Write/ Send rights of files belonging to the delegated account.*
3.	*Signature includes the name of both the users, ie. To whom charge is delegated and the user whose charge is delegated.*	*Signature includes the name of the user whose charge is delegated.*	*Signature includes the name of the user to whom charge is delegated.*
4.	*Movement History contains the name of the delegator as well as the delegated person.*	*Movement History contains the name of the user whose charge is delegated.*	*Movement History contains the name of the delegator as well as delegated person.*
5.	*This delegation is always with respect to an officer and not staff.* *There should be departmental instructions relating to such a provision.*	*This delegation is with respect to the personal staff attached to the officers.*	*This delegation is with respect to the link officers designated by the concerned department*

8. EXAMINING DOCUMENTS

8.1. Examination in Section by Dealing Hand:

8.1.1. When the line of action on a document is obvious or is based on a clear precedent or practice, or has been indicated by a higher officer, and a communication has to be issued, a draft should be put up without any elaborate note. In other cases, the dealing officer, while submitting a note on the case, should:

(i) see whether all the statements, so far as they are open to check, are correct;

(ii) point out mistakes, incorrect statements, missing data or information, if any;

(iii) obtain the missing and /or correct information from the sources concerned either over phone or using correspondence handling category of functional approach to noting;

(iv) furnish other relevant data or information available in the organization, if any;

(v) Prepare a note based on functional approach to noting (para 7.12(especially use of standard process sheet

(vi) state the issues for consideration and bring out clearly the points requiring decision;

(vii) Draw attention, if necessary, to the statutory or customary procedure and point out the relevant provisions of the Act, rules, instructions to the given case.

(viii) draw attention to precedents, if any,

(ix) Suggest the course of action to be taken with justification(s) along with alternative courses of action for consideration of the competent authority.

(x) Indicate the authority competent to take decision along with the copy of the delegation of powers

(xi) Affix full signature with complete date (DD/MM/YYYY) on the left below the note.

(xii) Leave space not less than one quarter of a page below the last recorded note on the note sheet of the file, especially when the file is submitted to the Secretary or Minister.

E-file

In e-file, with every note the dealing officers' signature consisting of his full name and post is appended to the noting along with date and time.

8.2 Examination by Section Officer:

Examination by Section Officer will include:

(i) Check if technique of functional approach to noting (para 7.14) has been adopted.

(ii) Consider possibility of using Standard Process Sheet either by using an existing Standard Process Sheet or developing a new one.

(iii) Evaluate adequacy and relevance of inputs provided

(iv) Section Officer and above are to simply sign, on the right side below the note with date, month and year (dd/mm/yyyy) if they agree with Section note. Else they are to record their note. Signature is to be rubber stamped.

8.3 Examination by Branch Officer and above

(i) A branch officer or Division-in-Charge or Wing-in-charge will discuss wherever necessary, with his team to decide the course of action to be taken on a case involving a new or a complex matter.

(ii) For dealing with such problem solving or policy cases, the technique of writing a discussed note may be used. Discussed note is submitted as a draft. After clearance from the senior officers, it is faired and submitted by the Dealing Officer

After discussion, the Dealing Hand is entrusted with preparing a comprehensive / self-contained note which will be put up to decision making level clearly indicating that it is a discussed note. Such discussed note shall also be a reasoned note based on the provisions of the relevant Act, rules, instructions, etc. The note will contain the background to the problem, issues arising out of the precedents, if any, analysis of all relevant facts with reference to the provisions of the relevant Act, Rules and /or guidelines, and the recommended course of action for approval by the competent authority.

E-file

In e-file, sending/ marking of receipts/ files are flexible. The system allows the user to send a receipt/ file to any other user and the movement of record is maintained (who has sent, to whom has been sent and when has been sent). Physical file which is marked to another officer has to be received by him/her by clicking appropriate buttons in his / her inbox, indicating that the physical file has been received at his/her end. The acknowledgement for the same should be obtained from the recipient.

Electronic file once marked to the next user goes to his/her inbox indicating that it has been received by him/her.

9. **AIDS TO PROCESSING OF CASES:** The dealing hand should, with the help of file registers, indices and aids to processing, such as standing guard file, standing note, precedent book, reference folders etc., locate and collect other files or papers, if any, referred to in the document, or having a bearing on the issues raised thereon. These aids are described below:

9.1 **Standing Guard File** on a subject means compilation consisting the following three parts:

(a) a running summary of the principles and policy relating to the subject, with number and date of relevant decisions or orders quoted in the margin against each;

(b) copies of the decisions or orders referred to, arranged in chronological order; and

(c) model forms of communications to be used at different stages.

9.2 **Standing note** in relation to a subject means a continuing note explaining, among other things, the history and development of the policy and procedure, designed to serve as:

(a) a complete background material for review of the existing policy or procedure,

(b) a brief for preparing replies to Parliament Questions or notes for supplementaries thereto; and

(c) induction or training material.

9.3 **Precedent Book** is a book for keeping note of important rulings and decisions having a precedent value for ready reference.

9.4 **Reference folder** in relation to a particular subject means a folder containing copies of relevant rules, orders, instructions etc., arranged in chronological order.

9.5 **Running summary of Facts** is a running summary of the facts of a case updated from time to time to incorporate changes whenever further developments take place. It also includes the advice or views of other organizations consulted in the matter but not opinions of individual officers within an organization. The summary may help in considering the case and avoids the need for repeated recapitulation of facts. It is placed on the file in a separate folder labeled as such in every case in which it is clear that such a summary would contribute to its speedy disposal.

10. DEVIATION FROM NORMAL PROCEDURES OR RULES

10.1 In every case where a major or minor infraction, other than trivial, of the existing procedures or rules, is sought to be made, it shall be the responsibility of the decision making authority to ensure that reasons are recorded in writing, justifying such a deviation from the rules or procedures.

11 ORAL DISCUSSIONS

11.1 All points emerging from discussions (including telephonic discussions) between two or more officers of different organizations, and the conclusions reached should be recorded on the relevant file by the officer authorizing action.

11.2 All discussions/instructions/decisions which the officer recording them considers to be important enough for the purpose, should be got confirmed by all those who have participated in or are responsible for them. This is particularly desirable in cases where the policy is not clear or where some important deviation from the prescribed policy is involved or where two or more levels differ on significant issues or the decision itself, though agreed upon by all concerned, is an important one.

11.3 Oral instructions by higher officers

11.3.1 Where an officer is giving direction (including telephonic direction) for taking action in any case in respect of matters on which he or his subordinate has powers to decide, he shall ordinarily do so in writing. If, however, the circumstances of the case are such that there is no time for giving the instructions in writing, he should follow it up by a written confirmation at his earliest.

11.3.2 An officer shall, in the performance of his official duties, or in the exercise of the powers conferred on him, act in his best judgement except when he is acting under instructions of an official superior. In the latter case, he shall obtain the directions in writing wherever practicable before carrying out the instructions, and where it is not possible to do so, he shall obtain written confirmation of the directions as soon thereafter as possible. If the officer giving the instructions is not his immediate superior but one higher to the latter in the hierarchy, he shall bring such instructions to the notice of his immediate superior at the earliest

11.4 Oral orders on behalf of or from the highest authority of the organization

11.4.1 Whenever a member of the personal staff of the highest authority of the organisation communicates to any officer an oral order on behalf of such authority, it shall be confirmed by him in writing immediately thereafter.

11.4.2 If any officer receives oral instructions from the highest authority or from his personal staff and the orders are in accordance with the norms, rules, regulations or procedures, they should be brought to the notice of the administrative head of the organization.

11.4.3 If any officer receives oral instructions from the highest authority or from his personal staff and the orders are not in accordance with the norms, rules, regulations or procedures, he should seek further clear orders from the administrative head of the organization about the line of action to be taken stating clearly that the oral instructions are not in accordance with the rules, regulations, norms or procedures.

11.4.4 In rare and urgent cases when the highest authority is on tour/ is sick and his approval has to be taken on telephone, the decision of the highest authority can be conveyed by his Private Secretary. In such cases, confirmation should be obtained on file when such authority returns to Headquarter/rejoins.

11.5 Confirmation of oral instructions

11.5.1 If an officer seeks confirmation of oral instructions given by his senior, the latter should confirm it in writing whenever such confirmation is sought.

11.5.2 Receipt of communications from Junior Officers seeking confirmation of oral instructions should be acknowledged by the Senior Officers or their personal staff, or the personal staff of the highest authority, as the case may be.

12. PUTTING UP OF THE CASES

12.1 Putting up of the case by the dealing hand

12.1.1 After identifying and examining issues involved in a case, the dealing hand should record a note, arrange and reference papers, attach a label indicating the urgency grading appropriate to the case, and put up the file to the Superintendent / Section officer. He should also mark the date of submission in col. 5 of the Assistant's Diary.

12.1.2 Papers for submission should be securely tied on a file board or a file flap.

12.1.3 The Superintendent / Section Officer should scrutinize the note of the dealing hand, record, where necessary, a note setting out his own comments or suggestions, and submit the case to the appropriate higher officer.

12.2 Arrangement of papers in a case

12.2.1 When submitting the case, the papers should be arranged in the following order from top downwards;

(i) reference books, if any;

(ii) notes portion of the current file ending with the note for consideration;

(iii) running summary of facts, if any;

(iv) draft for approval, if any;

(v) correspondence portion of the current file ending with the latest receipt or issue, as the case may be;

(vi) appendix to notes and appendix to correspondence, if any;

(vii) standing guard file, standing note or reference folder, if any;

(viii) other papers, if any, referred to, e.g., extracts of notes or correspondence from files, copies of orders, resolutions, gazettes, arranged in chronological order, the latest being placed on the top;

(ix) recorded files, if any, arranged in chronological order, the latest being placed on the top; and

(x) routine notes and papers arranged in chronological order and placed in a separate cover.

13 LINKING OF FILES

13.1 If the issues raised in two or more current files are so inter-connected that they must be dealt with together simultaneously, the relevant files should be linked in the manner indicated in 13.2 below.Such linking may also be resorted to if a paper on one current file is required for reference in dealing with another current file, unless a copy of the paper can be conveniently placed on the first file.

13.2 When files are to be linked, strings of the file board of the lower file (but not its flaps) should be tied around the upper file and those of the file board or flap of the upper file tied underneath it in a bow out of the way so that each file is intact with all its connected papers properly arranged on its file board or flap.

13.3 On receipt back after completion of action, the linked files should be immediately delinked after taking relevant extracts and placing them on the linked files, where necessary.

13.4 Use of urgency grading

13.4.1 The two urgency grading for use on cases are 'Immediate' and 'Priority'.

13.4.2 The label 'Immediate' should be used only in cases requiring prompt attention. Amongst the rest, the 'Priority' label should be used for cases which merit disposal in precedence to others of ordinary nature.

13.4.3 Where Lok Sabha / Rajya Sabha labels for questions, motions, bills are used, it is not necessary to use, in addition, 'Immediate' or 'Priority' label.

13.4.4 The grading of urgency assigned to a case should be reviewed by all concerned at different stages of its progress and, where necessary, revised. This is particularly important for cases proposed to be referred to other departments.

14. MODIFICATION OF NOTES OR ORDERS

14.1 Senior Officer should not require any modification in, or replacement of, the notes recorded by their juniors once they have been submitted to them. Instead, the higher officers should record their own notes giving their views on the subject, where necessary correcting or modifying the facts given in earlier notes. In any case, the replacement or modification of the notes which have already been recorded on a file, when the file has been further noted upon by others, should not be permitted.

14.2 Pasting over a note or a portion of it to conceal what has been recorded should not be done. Wherever a note recorded in the first instance requires any modification on account of additional facts or any error having come to notice, a subsequent note may be recorded, keeping the earlier note intact.

14.3 Where a final decision already communicated to a party is found later on to have been given on a mistaken ground or wrong facts or wrong interpretation of rules due to misunderstanding, such withdrawal may also have legal implications. In all such cases, in addition to consulting the Ministry of Law, wherever necessary, such a withdrawal should be permitted only after the approval of an officer higher than the one who took the original decision, has been obtained and reasons for the reversal or modification of the earlier decision have been duly recorded on the file.

15. NOTING ON FILES RECEIVED FROM OTHER DEPARTMENTS

15.1 If a reference seeks the opinion, ruling, or concurrence of the receiving department and requires detailed examination, such examination should normally be done separately through routine notes and only the final result should be recorded on the file by the officer responsible for commenting upon the reference. The officer to whom such a note is submitted will either accept that note or record a note of his own. In the former case, he may direct that the note in question or a specified portion thereof may be reproduced on the main file for communication to the department concerned. In the latter case, he should record a suitable note on the main file itself. In either case, a copy of the note recorded on the main file should be kept on the routine notes for retention in the receiving department before the file is returned to the originating department.

15.2 The department should open subject-wise files each year in which such routine notes should be kept. The inter-departmental note recorded on the file of the originating department should bear the subject file number to facilitate filing of papers and their retrieval for future reference.

15.3 Where the reference requires information of a factual nature or other action based on a clear precedent or practice, the dealing hand in the receiving department may note on the file straightaway.

15.4 Where a note on a file is recorded by an officer after obtaining the orders of a higher officer, the fact that the views expressed therein have the approval of the latter should be specifically mentioned.

15.5 In making written inter-departmental references, the following points should be observed:

(i) Inter-departmental references, should normally be made under the directions of an officer not below the rank of Under Secretary or as may be provided by the departmental instructions.

(ii) The points on which the opinion of other departments is sought or which it is desired to bring to their notice should be clearly stated.

(iii) Where possible, the drafts of the orders proposed to be issued may also be shown to the departments sought to be consulted.

(iv) When it is necessary to consult more than one department on a case, such consultation may be effected simultaneously by self-contained inter-departmental note, unless:

a. it involves copying of a large number of documents available on the file; or

b. the need for consulting the second department would arise only after the views of the first have become available.

15.6 When such a reference requires concurrence of one or more department the following further points should be observed;

(i) The originating department should invariably prescribe a time-limit when calling for comments or concurrence from other departments.

(ii) In case any of the departments so consulted is not in a position to send its comments/ concurrence within the prescribed time-limit, it should write back promptly, in any case before the prescribed time-limit, and indicate the additional time they would require for furnishing their final reply.

15.7 When such a reference does not require such concurrence, the originating department need not wait for the comments of other department beyond the prescribed time-limit, and it should feel free to go ahead with its scheme/ proposal without waiting any longer.

15.8 The initiating department should always feel free to recall its file from another department to which such a reference has been made on a file, if such a course is required to be adopted for expediting the process of decision making in the case.

Such a decision to recall a file should be taken at a level not lower than that of a branch officer in the originating department.

16. NOTING UNDER SINGLE FILE SYSTEM (SFS)

16.1 In the case of their own attached offices and subordinate offices placed directly under them, i.e. without the intervention of an attached office, as are located in Delhi / New Delhi – referred to herein as 'Non-Secretariat Organization' (NSO) - the departments should introduce the Single File System (SFS), the details of which are described in the following paragraphs.

16.2 This system will apply to matters which have to be referred by the NSO to the department for seeking a sanction / order, i.e. a decision not within its own delegated powers.

16.3 The file cover of an SFS case should prominently show the name of the (originating) NSO and likewise indicate that it follows the SFS system.

16.4 The SFS file need not bear an I.D. (Inter-Departmental) No. or other formal method of sending, but will be sent as though it is from one officer to another in the same organisation.

16.5 The SFS file should be complete in all respects, so as to enable the department to take a decision expeditiously. Hence the NSO should ensure that:

(i) every point for decision / order is clearly brought out;

(ii) all relevant connected papers are placed on the file, properly arranged and referred to;

(iii) draft orders / sanctions are put up, where they are required to be approved by the department for issue; and

(iv) the availability of funds, etc., is certified where additional expenditure is involved in the proposal.

16.6 The officer last dealing with the SFS case in the NSO should mark it to the appropriate officer in the department, by name. Policy files should, however, be referred to the department at appropriate levels to be determined by the department and the NSO concerned, through a general order.

16.7 All SFS file, should be invariably routed through the central registry of the department concerned. Their receipt should be entered in a separate register which should also record, against the relevant receipt entry, the dispatch of the file on its return to the NSO.

16.8 As a rule, all notings in the department should be on the NSO file. However, where sensitive or delicate matters in the sphere of personnel, policy issues, and finance are involved, the recording of notes in 'duplicate' file may be permitted by issuing general or special orders by the department. This should be done at a particular stage of the SFS case or at or above a particular level, with the final decision thereafter being suitably recorded on the SFS file.

16.9 As a convention, the secretariat noting on an SFS file should start on a new page and the noting done sequentially-except in matters of the nature referred to in para 10.8 above.

16.10 Action to implement the Government decision in SFS case, should be initiated in and by the NSO on the return of the file. Orders so issued should specifically state that they have received the concurrence of Government in the department concerned. Copies of every sanction/ order so issued by the NSO, should be endorsed without fail to all the officers concerned in the department.

16.11 The Single File System does not apply in dealings between a department and any statutory, corporate, or other autonomous body which might be owned or controlled by it.

17. CONCLUSION

Organizations today are like vast machines which work under great pressure. The work they perform has grown enormously in volume, complexity, and variety. In these circumstances, the need is for speedy disposal of work. Therefore, there is no scope today to indulge in unnecessary and repetitive notings on files. But the accountability and the answerability towards stakeholders require that there should be some record of the contributions made by functionaries at the different levels in the organization, and the circumstances and the considerations which led to the decisions that have been made. Notings in offices serve this vital need well.

EXERCISES

EXERCISE – 1

Fill in the blank in each of the following sentences by picking up the option, which you consider to be correct, from among those given below each sentence.

1. Noting is done on files to______________________

   (a) show the intellectual level of the persons writing notes.
   (b) delay disposal of cases so that importance of persons writing notes may be recognized.
   (c) facilitate disposal of cases.
   (d) justify multiple levels through which cases are processed.

2. When passing orders or making suggestions on the file, an officer should____________________________

   (a) repeat the points already made in previous notes so that the issues in a case could be high-lighted.
   (b) reproduce extracts from the paper under consideration.
   (c) confine his note to the actual points he proposes to make, without reiterating the ground already covered in the previous notes.
   (d) quote in full the relevant provisions of rules or instructions which have a bearing on the case.

3. In making written inter-departmental references, it should be ensured that the originating department________________________.

   (a) always makes such references only by self-contained notes so that the need for sending its file never arises.
   (b) where it is necessary to consult more than one department, such consultation is made simultaneously, even if the need for consulting the second department arises only after the views of the first department have become available.
   (c) clearly state the points on which the opinion of other departments is sought.
   (d) never prescribes time limit when calling for comments or concurrence from other departments.

4. When a paper under consideration raises several major points which require detailed examination____________.

(a) all these points should be examined in a single note on the file.

(b) each point should be noted upon separately in section notes.

(c) a major point should be examined first in the note on the file, and the next point should be examined after orders on the first point have been passed.

(d) the paper under consideration should be returned to the sender who may be asked to make separate references for each major point.

5. When a running summary of facts is available on a file, any officer who has to note upon a file should____________.

(a) draw attention to the facts of the case by referring to the appropriate part of the summary without repeating them in his note.

(b) repeat the facts in his note so that the need to refer to the summary does not arise.

(c) get a copy of the appropriate part of the summary and place it on the file.

(d) repeat verbatim the appropriate part of the summary in his note and make it self-contained.

6. Which of the following is true for an electronic file?

(a) Note can be added and referencing and docketing can be done using 'Add Green Note' option.

(b) With every note the dealing officers' Signature is appended to the noting along with date and time.

(c) Sending / marking of receipts / file is flexible.

(d) all of the above.

EXERCISE-2

Fill in the blank in each of the following sentences by picking up the option, which you consider to be correct, from among those given below each sentence.

1. A good note is one which________________________

(a) leaves some points unanswered so that personal discussion with the dealing hand becomes necessary.

(b) is written in abstract, flowery language and is full of long sentences.

(c) emphasises negative facts so that the case may be rejected.

(d) is concise and to the point free from wordy expressions.

2. Where a note recorded in the first instance requires any modification on account of additional facts or any error having come to notice it, is advisable that ________________.

(a) the note or a portion of it may be pasted over to conceal what had been recorded earlier.

(b) the earlier note is replaced by a fresh one.

(c) a fresh note is put up on a new file without any reference to the note recorded on the earlier file.

(d) a subsequent note is recorded, keeping the earlier note intact.

3. After examining a reference from a department seeking the opinion, ruling, or concurrence, the receiving department should ________________.

(a) record only the final result on the file.

(b) quote opinions of officers, who have examined the reference, in the note recorded on the file of the department making the reference.

(c) also send its routine notes to the department making the reference so that it can understand why a particular view was expressed by the receiving department.

(d) keep the file of the department making the reference and send only a self-contained note to it.

4. A good note should________________________________.

(a) be so organised that the reader could understand its contents only after reading it several times.

(b) convey the information needed in a case, even though its presentation is not visually attractive.

(c) express ideas tactfully without hurting anybody's feelings.

(d) express displeasure in strong language if incorrect statements have been made in a case.

5. Where a note is recorded by an officer after obtaining the orders of a higher officer____________________.

(a) the officer recording the note should claim that he has recorded the note on his own without any reference to higher officer.

(b) such higher officer should be requested to confirm his approval by signing the note on the file.

(c) the referring department should be advised to get the fact confirmed by such higher officer.

(d) the fact that the views expressed in the note have the approval of such higher officer should be specifically mentioned in the note.

EXERCISE - 3

1. The Staff Selection Commission (Government of India) is conducting a competitive examination for recruitment of Junior Engineers (Civil and Electrical) in February 2023 (vide advertisement No. A-44012/3-2022 dated 29.01.2022). The last date for receipt of applications in the Regional offices of the Commission is 25.2.2022.

2. Shri Makhan Lal, LDC in the Stores Section of the Power Development Corporation, (Ministry of Power, Government of India), Chandigarh, has submitted an application dated 03.02.2022, for appearing at this examination. You, as the dealing Assistant in Admn. I section of the Corporation, have been allotted this receipt for taking necessary action.

3. Please open a new file (A-44012/3-2022 -Admn. I) to deal with this application, and put up a note seeking approval for giving a 'No Objection Certificate' and forwarding the application to the Regional Office of the Commission at Chandigarh.

EXCERCISE - 4

1. Shri Jamna Das, Assistant in the Budget Section of the Central Roads and Infrastructure Development Corporation (Ministry of Transport, Government of India), has applied for grant of permission to join a one-year part-time course in Journalism being conducted by the Indira Gandhi National Open University (IGNOU), New Delhi. The application has been forwarded by the Superintendent in charge of the Budget Section.

2. You, as the dealing Assistant in Admn. I Section of the Corporation, have been allotted this receipt for necessary action. On enquiry, you have been informed that the Journalism Course will be conducted from July 2022 to June 2023. There will be two examinations-one half-yearly examination in December 2022, and a final examination in June 2023. The University will conduct contact classes for the benefit of the enrolled students on Tuesdays, Thursdays, and Saturdays from 5.00 P.M. to 7.00 P.M. each day, and attendance of students in these classes is compulsory.

3. The Corporation follows five-day week from Monday to Friday. Office timings are from 10.00 A.M. to 6.00 P.M.

4. Please open a new file (F No. A-20012/8-2022-Admn.I), and put up a note giving your recommendation.

EXERCISE – 5

1. The Administration I Section of the National Road Transport Corporation has to process a large number of applications about grant of leave to the employees of the Corporation. With a view to avoid repetitive noting and speed up disposal of work, it is proposed to introduce a standard process sheet for examining such applications.

2. Please prepare a standard process sheet for this purpose.

EXERCISE – 6

1. On the basis of the recommendations of the Union Public Service Commission, Shri Bimal Prakash, a Deputy Director in the Directorate of Health Services under the Department of Health, has been selected for appointment as a Joint Director (scale of pay: Rs. 12000 – Rs. 16500) in the Central Children Welfare Board under the Department of Social Development. The appointment will be on deputation for a maximum period of five years, but the initial appointment will be for a period of one year, extendable on year to year basis with mutual consent.

2. Please put up a note to obtain the Minister's approval to this appointment before it is notified.

EXERCISE – 7

1. Shri Vimal Prakash, an Under Secretary in the Department of Cultural Affairs, had applied for, and was granted, earned leave for 30 days from 2.1.2021 to 31.1.2021. He had mentioned in his leave application that during this leave he intended to visit his children who are settled in the U.S.A. He had also given his leave address in the application.

2. On 9.1.2021, the Department made a frantic search for Shri Vimal Prakash. The Department decided to recall Shri Vimal Prakash from leave, because his presence was urgently required in connection with preparations for the meeting of the Parliamentary Committee on Cultural Affairs. When told that Shri Vimal Prakash was not at his headquarters but had gone abroad, objections were raised to his leaving the headquarters without permission. Even disciplinary proceedings were contemplated against him for this "act of indiscipline." At that time, a suggestion was made to consult the Department of Personnel before initiating any such action.

3. Please prepare an inter-departmental (I.D.) note for the Department of Personnel.

EXERCISE – 8

The Himachal Pradesh Hydro-electric Projects Corporation, Sector 17, Chandigarh, had placed an order for the supply of 100 office chairs on M/S Newlook Furniture Works, Haiderpur. The Company had agreed to supply the chairs within one month from the date of issue of the letter. But, although two months have passed, the supply has not yet been made.

2. As the dealing Assistant in the Purchase Section of the Corporation, you intend to remind the Company to supply the chairs very early. Please put up a note (on F. No. 39/23/2021-PUR) stating the position and seeking approval for the action you propose to take.

EXERCISE – 9

Shri Krishna Kumar, Assistant Director, Institute of Secretariat Training was granted study leave for a period of 12 months from 1.7.2021 to 30.6.2022, for pursuing an Executive Development Programme at a Management Institute. He has sent an application requesting the grant of this study leave in two spells from 1.7.2021 to 30.11.2021 and from 1.1.2022 to 31.7.2022, because the Management Institute will be closed during the month of December 2021.

2. Please examine this request and put up a note (on. F. No. 21/8/2021-Admn. I) giving the recommendation you consider appropriate.

EXERCISE – 10

The Central Roads & Infrastructure Development Corporation has its headquarters at New Delhi. It has 1000 employees; of these, 600 employees are in 15 field offices spread over the country, and 400 employees are at the headquarters. The Corporation follows a policy of involving its employees in the decision-making process. It has set up a Staff Council at the headquarters. The Council has 20 members, of whom 75 per cent are elected from among the employees in the field offices; 20 per cent by employees at the headquarters; and 5 per cent are nominated by the Chairman of the Corporation. The Chairman presides over the meetings of the Staff Council. The Chief Welfare Officer is the Secretary of the Council.

2. The Staff Council has, in its meeting held on 23 April 2021, passed a Resolution (copy attached) recommending grant of merit scholarships to the children of employees with a view to encouraging them to pursue higher studies. This Resolution has been sent to Admn. II section by the Secretary of the Council through a letter dated 26.4.2021. It has been allotted to you for taking action.

3. Please open a new file (No. 32/5/2021-Admn II), and put up the Resolution as a PUC on the file. Also write a note examining the receipt, and giving your recommendation.

Note 1 – The Chairman has the powers to sanction expenditure on welfare measures up to Rs. 5 lakhs in each case.

Note 2 – Funds are available in the budget to meet expenditure on the grant of scholarships.

ENCLOSURE

The Staff Council of the Central Roads and Infrastructure Development Corporation passed the following Resolution in the meeting held on 23 April 2021:

RESOLUTION

RESOLVED that with a view to recognizing merit and encouraging children of the employees of the Corporation to pursue higher studies in recognised and approved institutions, the Council recommends that:

(1) The Corporation should grant 10 scholarships each year to those children who obtain 90 per cent or more marks in the aggregate in the Senior Secondary School Examination for Class XII.

(2) Each scholarship will be of the value of Rs. 500 per month. In the case of students in the Arts, Commerce, and Science streams, the scholarships will be for a period of three years initially, extendable by another two years for those students who pursue post graduate courses (including Management Courses) in these streams. In the case of students in medical, architecture, technical, and law streams, the scholarships will be for the duration of the course, subject to a maximum of five years.

(3) An annual grant of Rs. 5,000 will be given to each student for meeting expenditure on books required for the studies.

ANSWERS

EXERCISE - 1

1. (c) 2. (c) 3. (c) 4. (b) 5. (a) 6. (d)

EXERCISE - 2

1. (d) 2. (d) 3. (a) 4. (c) 5. (d)

EXERCISE - 3

POWER DEVELOPMENT CORPORATION (Ministry of Power) Admn. I Section
F. No. A-44012/3-2022 – Admn. I
SUJBJECT FORWARDING OF APPLICATIONS FOR POSTS OUTSIDE THE CORPORATION

S. No. 1 (Receipt)– Application dated 3.2.2022 from Shri Makhan Lal, LDC, Stores Section

Shri Makhan Lal, LDC, Stores Section, has submitted an application in response to the advertisement issued by the Staff Selection Commission (Government of India) for recruitment of Junior Engineers (Civil and Electrical) through a competitive examination. The last date for reaching the applications in the Regional Offices of the Commission is 25.02.2022.

2. Shri Makhan Lal is a temporary employee who was appointed on 14.3.2022.

3. Vigilance section have certified p.6/c that no disciplinary proceedings are pending or contemplated against Shri Makhan Lal.

4. Shri Makhan Lal's application may be forwarded to the Regional Office of the Staff Selection Commission at Chandigarh. The No Objection Certificate printed on the application p 4/c form may also be signed.

sd/-

(Chetan Das)

08.02.2022

Supdt. (Admn),

EXERCISE - 4

CENTRAL ROADS and INFRASTRUCTRURE DEVELOPMENT CORPORATION (Ministry of Transport) Admn. I Section
F. No. A-20012/8/2022 – Admn. I
SUBJECT Application for grant of permission to attend part – time courses

S. No. 1 (Receipt p.u.c. pp. 1-2/c) – Application dated 3.3.2022 from Shri Jamna Das, Asstt. Budget Section.

1. **Proposal** – Shri Jamna Das, Assistant, Budget Section, has applied p.u.c. for permission to attend one-year part time course in Journalism being conducted by IGNOU from July 2022 to June 2023. His application has been forwarded by the Superintendent of Budget Section.

2. **Details of the course** – IGNOU will conduct contact classes for the benefit of enrolled students on Tuesdays, Thursdays and Saturdays from 5.00 P.M. to 7.00 P.M. each day. Attendance of students enrolled for this course is compulsory. There will be a half-yearly examination in December 2022, and a final examination in June 2023.

3. **Recommendation of Budget Section** – Shri Jamna Das's application has been forwarded by Superintendent of the Budget Section. The Superintendent has, however, not given his recommendation. When contacted on this point, the Superintendent clarified that it is for the Administration Section to allow Shri Jamna Das to attend the part time course or not. On his part, however, he said that he would be able to manage the work somehow in case Shri Jamna Das is granted permission on the week days when Shri Jamna Das may not be available when he may be attending contact classes or, in case he takes leave for preparing for examinations during December 2022 and June 2023. Similar views were expressed by the Manager, Budget Division, when he was asked to give his recommendation.

4. **Implications of the request** – In case Shri Jamna Das is allowed to join the part time course and attend contact classes, he may have to leave early, say by 4.00 p.m., so that he can reach the venue of the classes. While we may have no objection to his attending contact classes on Saturdays on which days the office is closed, attending classes on Tuesdays and Thursdays would mean that he should be allowed to leave by 4.00 p.m. on these days, i.e., at least 2 hours earlier than the closing time. This would be against office discipline.

5. Similarly, Shri Jamna Das may ask for leave for preparing for the examinations in December 2022, and June 2023. Depending upon the need of services during these times, it would be difficult commit the grant of leave for preparing and appearing at the examinations during the months.

6. **Alternatives and their implications** – The following alternatives may be considered when making a decision on Shri Jamna Das's request:

1. Shri Jamna Das may be allowed to attend the part time course in Journalism.

   It means we agree to his leaving office early on Tuesday's and Thursdays, and grant him leave, when requested, for preparing and appearing at the examinations. His leaving office early will undermine office discipline, and granting him leave may adversely affect office work. Besides, it will be difficult to resist similar demands from other employees. Also, no commitment can be given about grant of leave in connection with the examinations.

2. Shri Jamna Das may not be allowed to join the part time course in Journalism.

   It will give a wrong message to other employees that we do not care for their welfare. We would be projected as a heartless organization in not giving chances to our employees to improve their qualifications and better their prospects. Besides, we would also lose an opportunity to have a qualified person among our staff, who can help in presenting a better image of our Corporation. Employees may also decide to agitate to set the "wrong" "right".

3. Shri Jamna Das may be posted in the morning shift from 8.00 a.m. to 4.00 p.m. in the Receipt and Issue Section. This Section works in two shifts-one from 8.00 a.m. to 4.00 p.m. and the other from 12.00 noon to 8.00 p.m. An Assistant from Receipt

and Issue Section may be transferred to Budget Section as substitute for Shri Jamna Das. In this way, the question of his leaving office early will not arise because he will be able to leave by 4.00 p.m. every day. No disruption of work is likely to be caused if he is granted leave during the examination periods. The work in Budget Section is likely to remain unaffected, because that Section is prepared to manage work with whoever substitute is provided in place of Shri Jamna Das.

7. **Recommendations** – It is suggested that Shri. Jamna Das may be transferred to Receipt and Issue Section to work in the morning shift from 8.00 a.m. to 4.00 p.m., and an Assistant from Receipt and issue section may be transferred to Budget Section.

It is also suggested that Shri Jamna Das may be granted permission to join the part time course in journalism being conducted by IGNOU from July 2022 to June 2023.

8. **Approval** – Approval of Chairman may be obtained to do the recommendations made in para 7 above.

Sd/- Chiranji Lal

16.03.2022

Supdt. (Admn. I)

EXERCISE – 5

STANDARD PROCESSING SHEET

APPLICATION FOR LEAVE OR FOR EXTENSION OF LEAVE

1. Name:
2. Post Held:
3. Division / Office / Section:
4. Basic pay and Scale of pay:
5. House rent and other compensatory allowances drawn in the present post:
6. Nature and period of leave applied for and the date from which required.
7. Sundays and holidays, if any, proposed to be prefixed / suffixed to leave:
8. Purpose for which leave is required:
9. Date of return from last leave, and the nature and period of that leave:
10. Will leave travel concession for the block years _____ be availed of during the leave applied for? Yes / No*
11. Address during leave:

Signature of Applicant

Date______________________

* Strike out which is not applicable

REMARKS / RECOMMENDATION OF CONTROLLING OFFICER

12. Will a substitute be required during the applicant's absence on leave?

13. Remarks and / or recommendation of the Controlling Officer.

Signature

Designation_______________

Date _______________

REMARKS / RECOMMENDATION OF ESTABLISHMENT / ADMINISTRATION DIVISION

14. Is the leave applied for admissible?

15. Is the information is col. 9 above correct?

16. Will the arrangement for posting a substitute (if required) be made?

17. Recommendation

Signature_______________

Designation_______________

Date _______________

ORDERS OF THE COMPETENT AUTHORITY

Leave applied for is granted / not granted

Signature_______________

Designation_______________

Date _______________

EXERCISE – 6

1. **Proposal** – A Post of Joint Director (scale of pay Rs. 12000 – Rs. 16500) will fall vacant in the Central Children Welfare Board on 1st February 2023, consequent on the repatriation of the present incumbent to his parent department on 31st January 2023. It is proposed to fill up this post.

2. **Provisions in Recruitment Rules and action taken** – According to the recruitment rules, this post is required to be filled in consultation with the Union Public Service Commission, on transfer on deputation of suitable officers with five years' service in a post in the scale of pay of Rs. 10000 – 12000. We had initiated the process of filling up this post in November 2022 itself, so that the selected person could be in position on 1.2.2023.

3. **Recommendation of UPSC** – The Union Public Service Commission have recommended the name of Shri Bimal Prakash, presently a Deputy Director in the Directorate of Health Services under the Department of Health for appointment to the post of Joint Director in the Central Children Welfare Board.

4. **Certificate** – Department of Health have certified that no vigilance or disciplinary case is pending or contemplated against Shri Bimal Prakash.

5. **Terms of appointment** – Shri Bimal Prakash's appointment will be on transfer on deputation for a period of five years. However, his appointment will be for one year initially, extendable on year to year basis for a maximum period upto five years with mutual consent.

6. **Approval** – Approval of the Minister may be obtained to the appointment of Shri Bimal Prakash on the terms stated in para 5 above, before the appointment is notified.

Sd/- Rama Shankar

16.1.2023

SO (CW)

EXERCISE - 7

Government of India

DEPARTMENT OF CULTURAL AFFAIRS

Subject: Requirement of taking prior permission by Government servants for leaving station/ headquarters.

1. **The Problem** – An officer of this Department had applied for, and was granted, earned leave for thirty days from 2.1.2022 to 31.1.2022. He had mentioned in his leave application that he intended to visit his children, who are settled in a foreign country, during this leave. He had also given his leave address in the foreign country.

2. After the officer had proceeded on leave, his presence was required for attending to some urgent official work. But, when it was found that the officer was not in his headquarters, a question was raised whether it was proper for him to leave headquarters without permission, and if not, whether a serious view of his absence from headquarters can be taken and disciplinary action initiated against him.

3. **Provision in the rules** – Under the provisions of F.R. 11, the whole time of a Government servant is at the disposal of the Government. Similar provision has been made in the Civil Service Regulations, and Article 56 of these regulations provides that no officer is entitled to any pay and allowances for any time he may spend beyond the limits of his charge without authority. According to these provisions, it is essential that a Government servant should obtain permission for leaving station / headquarters, particularly when he proposes to go abroad.

4. **Question for consideration** – In the context explained above, the following questions have arisen:

(1) Whether the government servant, who was granted leave, should have obtained permission for leaving headquarters before proceeding on leave, although he had stated in his leave application that he will go abroad during his leave?

(2) If so, whether it is a fit case for initiating disciplinary action against him for his failure to obtain permission before leaving his headquarters?

5. **The request**- This Department will be grateful for the advice of the Department of Personnel on the questions raised in para 4 above.

Sd/- (Vidya Sagar)

Deputy Secretary

Tel. No. 23011326

Department of Personnel (Shri M.M. Krishnan, Dy. Secy.)

North Block, New Delhi

Department of Cultural Affairs I.D. No. 15/3/2022 – Admn. I dated 16.1.2022

EXERCISE – 8

(Note to be recorded on F. No. 39/23/2021-PUR)

In our letter dated 9.1.2021, we had placed an order for the supply of 100 office chairs with M/s New look Furniture Works, Haiderpur. These chairs were to be supplied within one month from the date of issue of the letter, as per agreement with the company. But these chairs have not been supplied, although two months have passed since the order was placed.

2. We may remind the firm to supply the office chairs immediately.

sd/-
(Ravi Parkash)
10.3.2021

Supdt. (Pur)

EXERCISE –9

(Note to be recorded on F. No. 21/8/2021-Admn I)

S. No. 4 (Receipt) – Application dated 3.8.2021 from Shri Krishna Kumar, Asstt. Dir.

1. **Introduction** – Shri Krishna Kumar, Assistant Director, was granted a study leave of twelve months from 1.7.2021 to 30.6.2022 for pursuing an Executive Development Programme being conducted by the Modern Management Institute, New Delhi.

2. **Request** – Shri Kumar has requested that the study leave may be granted in two spells-one from 1.7.2021 to 30.11.2021, and another from 1.1.2022 to 31.7.2022-because the Modern Management Institute will be closed during December 2021.

3. **Rule Position** – Under Rule 51 of the Central Civil Services (Leave) Rules, 1972, the study leave can be granted ordinarily for twelve months at any one time and during the entire service, 24 months in all. The Government's decision below this rule also clarifies that study leave may be availed of in more than one spell, provided such study leave availed of in different spells does not exceed 24 months.

4. **Justification** – The request of Shri Kumar seems to be justified, and there may be no objection to accepting this request. There is no point is Shri Kumar wasting one month when the Institute will be closed and extend the period of study leave by one month to enable him to complete the course in July 2022.

5. **Suggestion** – We may request the Department of Personnel to approve the proposal to permit Shri Kumar to avail of the study leave in two spells from 1.7.2021 to 30.11.2021, and from 1.1.2022 to 31.7.2022. During the month of December 2021, Shri Kumar will work in our Institute.

6. **Approval** - Director may kindly accord his approval, where-after the file may be referred to the Department of Personal for their approval under SFS.

Sd/-
(Kripa Shankar)
5.8.2021

S.O. (Admn.).

EXERCISE – 10

CENTRAL ROADS & INFRASTRUCTURE DEVELOPMENT CORPORATION (Ministry of Transport) Admn. II Section
F. No. 32/5/2021 – Admn. II
SUBJECT Grant of merit scholarships to the children of employees of the Corporation.

S. No. 1 (Receipt) - Letter dated 26.4.2021 from the Secretary, Staff Council, Central Roads & Infrastructure Development Corporation.

1. **Proposal** – Secretary, Staff Council of our Corporation, has sent a copy of the Resolution passed by the Staff Council on 23.4.2021 about the grant of merit scholarships to children of employees of the Corporation. These scholarships will be granted to those children who obtain 90% or more marks in the Senior Secondary School Examination for Class XII. According to the Resolution, 10 scholarships, each of which will be of Rs. 500/- per month, will be granted every year. In the case of students in the Arts, Commerce, and Science streams, the scholarships will be for a period of three years initially, extendable by another two years for those students who pursue post graduate courses (including management courses) in these streams. In the case of students in medical, architecture, technical, and law streams, the scholarships will be for the duration of the course, subject to a maximum of five years. An annual book grant of Rs. 5000/- each will also be given to the students.

2. **Why the proposal?** The proposal is a welfare measure for employees and an attempt to recognize meritorious children, and encourage them to pursue higher studies. The proposed scholarships and grant are not intended to meet all the expenditure such children may incur on their studies, but it will certainly help in meeting some part of the expenditure. The proposal also reflects the feeling that the Corporation cares for its employees.

3. **Implications of the proposal** - Assuming that in the first year, 10 students will be awarded scholarships and the annual book grant and, as they move up, successive batches of students will be similarly awarded, the total number of students during the five-year period and also during the subsequent years will be 50, as shown below:

1st year	=	10	=	10
2nd year	=	10 + 10	=	20

3rd year	=	10 + 10 + 10	=	30
4th year	=	10 + 10 + 10 + 10	=	40
5th year	=	10 + 10 + 10 + 10 + 10	=	50

In subsequent years, the number will remain 50, as one batch will move out on completion of 5 years and a new batch will come in.

4. The expenditure on scholarships and book grants will be :

		Scholarship	Book Grant	Total
		Rs.	Rs.	Rs.
1st year	=	10 x 6000 = 60000	10 x 5000 = 50000	1,10,000
2nd year	=	20 x 6000 = 1,20,000	20 x 5000 = 1,00,000	2,20,000
3rd year	=	30 x 6000 = 1,80,000	30 x 5000 = 1,50,000	3,30,000
4th year	=	40 x 6000 = 2,40,000	40 x 5000 = 2,00,000	4,40,000
5th year	=	50 x 6000 = 3,00,000	50 x 5000 = 2,50,000	5,50,000

and it will be Rs. 5,50,000 in each of the subsequent years. But, Chairman is competent to sanction uptoRs. 5,00,000 only in each case. The estimated expenditure will, therefore, be beyond his competence in the fifth year and beyond.

5. **Alternatives** – To ensure that the expenditure remains within Chairman's competence, the following alternatives may be considered:

(1) Reduce the amount of scholarships and retain the book grant as proposed.

(2) Retain the proposed amount of scholarships but reduce the amount of book grant.

(3) Reduce the number of scholarships and book grants but keep the amount as proposed.

(4) Retain the number and amount of scholarships as proposed but give a little reduced book grant on graded basis i.e. a minimum amount of Rs. 800/- in the first year, Rs. 1600/- in the second year, Rs. 2400/- in the third year, Rs. 3200/- in the fourth year, and Rs. 4000/- in the fifth year.

6. **Implications of the alternatives** – All these alternatives are likely to be unacceptable to the staff side, because acceptance of any alternative will mean either lesser number of scholarships or reduced amount of these scholarships and book grants. But, of these, the alternative (4) is likely to be least resisted. Under this alternative, the

number of scholarships and their amount is not being reduced. As for book grant, the expenditure on books is likely to be less in the first year, but as the studies progress, more expenditure on books may be necessary, and it is likely to be maximum in the fifth year, when the amount of Rs. 4000/- is proposed to be sanctioned. The expenditure will also be within Chairman's competence, as shown below:

	Scholarship Rs.	Book grant Rs.	Total Rs.
1st year	60,000	8000	68,000
2nd year	1,20,000	24,000 (8000+16000)	1,44,000
3rd year	1,80,000	48,000 (8000+16000+24000)	2,28,000
4th year	2,40,000	80,000 (8,000+16,000+24,000+32,000)	3,20,000
5th year and beyond	3,00,000	1,20,000 (8,000+16,000+24,000+32,000+40,000)	4,20,000

7. **Recommendation** – It is suggested that alternative (4) in para 5 may be approved. Thereafter, the staff side may also be consulted and their agreement obtained. Further details about eligibility, mode of disbursement, monitoring of the students, progress etc. will be worked out after the agreement of the staff side has been obtained.

8. **Approval** – Chairman's approval to the recommendation in para 7 above may be obtained.

Sd/- Lalit Narayan
30.4.2021

Supdt. (Admn. II)

Chapter - Seven

DRAFTING

1. INTRODUCTION

1.1 After a decision has been made in a case, action is taken to convey it to the party concerned through an appropriate form of communication. In some cases, in which the branch officer or a higher officer has formulated his ideas, he may prepare a communication and authorise it for issue. In other cases, a draft is prepared and put up for approval of the competent authority.

1.2 In this chapter, we shall discuss how drafting is done and what points should be taken care of while drafting communications.

2. WHAT IS DRAFTING?

2.1 A *draft* is a rough copy of the communication which is intended to be issued to convey decision or decisions or views of the competent authority. *Drafting* is the process of preparing this rough copy.

2.2 A draft is prepared on behalf of the competent authority. It is intended to convey the decision or views of the competent authority in such a way as if such authority has written the communication himself. Thus, the time and effort of the competent authority are saved, and he could give more attention to other important and urgent matters.

3. CASES WHERE DRAFTING IS NOT REQUIRED

3.1 In routine cases, such as acknowledgements, reminders, enquiries, or replies to enquiries, and when non-confidential nature of information is to be obtained or conveyed, drafting is not required. In such cases pre-printed form letters are used.

3.2 No drafting is required in cases of simple and straightforward nature or those of repetitive nature for which standard forms of communication exist. In such cases, fair copies of the communication may be submitted to the appropriate officer for signature.

4. PROCEDURE FOR DRAFTING

4.1 It is not always necessary to await the approval of the proposed line of action and the draft should be put up simultaneously along with the notes by the initiating level officer. The higher officer may revise the draft if it does not conform to the approved course of action.

4.2 After a final decision is taken by the competent authority, he may have the fair communication made for his signature and authorise its issue; otherwise, he should prepare a draft and submit it to the appropriate higher officer for approval.

4.3 The officer approving the issue of a draft should append his initials with the date on the draft. It is also expected of him that he passes order on the file simultaneously whether the draft so approved should be kept on the file (along with the office copy of the communication issued in fair) or not.

4.4 Initial drafting should be done in black or blue ink. Modification in the draft at the subsequent levels may be made in green or red ink by the officers so as to distinguish the corrections made.

5. GUIDELINES FOR DRAFTING

a. A draft should carry the message sought to be conveyed in a language that is clear, concise, and incapable of misconstruction.

b. Lengthy sentences, abruptness, redundancy, circumlocution, superlatives and repetition, whether of words, observations or ideas, should be avoided.

c. Official communications emanating from a department and purporting to convey the laws or orders of the Government must specifically be expressed to have been written under the directions of Government. This requirement does not, however, imply that each communication should start with the phrase 'I am directed to say' or 'The undersigned is directed to convey', which has the effect of distancing the communicator from the reader at the very outset. A more direct and to-the-point format is to be preferred if some degree of rapport is to be established with the receiver of the communication. The obligatory requirement can be met in a variety of imaginative ways. For instance, variations of the phrase can be added to the operative part of the letter towards the end as under:

i. "............. I have the pleasure to inform you that the government, on reconsideration of the matter, has decided to sanction an additional grant of ...."

or

ii. "............... In the light of the above developments, government conveys its inability to accede to ...."

d. Communications of some length or complexity should generally conclude with a summary.

e. While asking for information, comments from the addressee, specify the data by which they are required, For example, Instead of stating, ".. maybe sent immediately." State. "... maybe sent by 28.02.2022.

E-file

In the e-file system, there is a provision for creating a draft in a template. Also the draft created in word can be uploaded directly to the system. There are other ways like typing directly on the editor of the draft and using copy and paste function from a compatible source.

f. Depending upon the form of communication, the subject should be mentioned in it (including reminders). The form of communication should be selected after looking at the nature of the content to be communicated.

g. The number and date of the last communication in the series, and if this is not from the addressee, his last communication on the subject, should always be referred to. Where it is necessary to refer to more than one communication or a series of communications, this should be done in the margin of the draft.

h. All drafts put up on a file should bear the file number. When two or more communications are to be issued from the same file to the same addressee on the same date, a separate serial number may be inserted before the numeral identifying the year to avoid confusion in reference, e.g.,A-1101/5/(I)/2021-Est., A-1101/5(II)/2021-Est.

i. A draft should clearly specify the enclosures which are to accompany the fair copy. In addition, short oblique lines should be drawn at appropriate places in the margin for ready reference by the typist, the comparers and the dispatcher. The number of enclosures should also be indicated at the end of the draft on the bottom left of the page thus- 'Encl.3'.

j. If copies of an enclosure referred to in the draft are available and are, therefore, not to be typed, an indication to that effect should be given in the margin of the draft below the relevant oblique line.

k. If the communication to be dispatched by post is important (e.g.,a notice cancelling a license or withdrawing an existing facility) or encloses a valuable document (such as an agreement, service book or a cheque) instructions as to whether it should be sent through registered post or speed post or in an insured cover, should be given on the draft by the Superintendent/Section Officer concerned with its issue.

l. Urgent communication with bulky enclosures to far-flung areas like Andaman and Nicobar Islands should be arranged to be dispatched by Air Parcel through Indian Airlines. The addressee should also be advised through wireless to take delivery of the consignment. Instructions to this effect should be given by the Divisional Head / Branch Officer/Section Officer at the time of approval of draft.

m. The name, designation, telephone number, fax number, and e-mail address of the officer, over whose signature the communication is to be issued, should invariably be indicated on the draft.

n. In writing, or typing a draft, sufficient space should be left on the margin and between successive lines so that additions or interpolation of words may be made, if necessary.

o. A slip bearing the words 'Draft for approval' should be attached to the draft. If two or more drafts are put up on a file, the drafts as well as the slips attached thereto should be marked 'DFAI', DFA II', 'DFA III' and so on.

p. Drafts which are to be issued as 'Immediate' or 'Priority' should be so marked under the orders of an officer not lower in rank than a Superintendent/ Section Officer.

> ***E-file***
>
> ***In the e-file system, there is a provision for initiating a draft at any level in the hierarchy and getting it approved and signed by any level with a pre-defined approver and signatory role respectively.***
>
> ***There is also a provision to initiate a draft without a file in case of receipts received.***
>
> ***Once the draft is approved, no change can be made in the draft content by any authority. There is also option for appending e-Sign/ Digital signature by the signatory. If necessary, the file has to be resubmitted for amendment of the approved draft.***

6. AUTHENTICATION OF GOVERNMENTS ORDERS

6.1 All orders and other instruments made and executed in the name of the President should be expressed to be made in his name and signed by an officer having regular or ex-officio secretariat status of and above the rank of Under Secretary, or other officer specifically authorized to authenticate such orders.

6.2 Where the power to make orders, notifications, etc., is conferred by a statute on the Government of India, such orders and notifications should be expressed to be made in the name of the Government of India.

7. ADDRESSING COMMUNICATIONS TO OFFICERS BY NAME

Normally, no communication, other than that of a classified nature or a demi-official letter, should be addressed or marked to an officer by name, unless it is intended that the matter raised therein should receive his personal attention either because of its special nature, urgency or importance, or because some ground has already been covered by personal discussion with him and he would be in a better position to deal with it. In such cases, the communication is to be addressed to the Head of the organization and "Attention: Shri XYZ, …." is written above the subject".

8. DRAFTING OF DEMI-OFFICIAL LETTERS

8.1 As the objective of writing a demi-official (d.o.) letter is to call the personal attention of the addressee, the style of writing should be direct, personal and friendly. More usage of active voice is to be preferred. (**e.g.** 'I notice' rather than 'It is noticed'). It is expedient to come to the issue at the beginning itself e.g. 'I seek your cooperation in the matter of ....'

8.2 A demi-official (d.o.) letter should preferably not exceed one page. If the message to be conveyed is lengthy, it is better to condense it into one page in a few small and meaningful paragraphs in a manner that holds the interest of the addressee; the detailed arguments can be set out in appendices.

8.3 The colour code in demi-official (d.o.) letter will be as follows: a demi-official (d.o.) letter from a Minister will exhibit the National Emblem in blue colour and that from an officer will exhibit the National Emblem in red colour.

E-file

(i) ***In e-file, the issue can be made electronically through emails and an office copy of the issue gets automatically attached to the file along with any enclosures sent. In e-file, fairing of approved drafts is not required as it is automatically done by the system at every level of correction/ editing/ contribution.***

(ii) ***Therefore, at the initial stage itself, the draft is prepared as necessary for issue from amongst the formats available.***

(iii) ***In e-file, the dispatch is made electronically as well as manually and all data relating to the issue is saved in the system. In case of electronic dispatch of e-files, it can be done directly from one officer to another through the e-file system. However, for such a movement to take place, both the offices should be working in the e-Office environment.***

(iv) ***In e-file, the signatory signs the approved draft with his digital signature/ e-Sign.***

(v) ***In e-file, the dispatch of communication can be done through email.***

(vi) ***And in return it should be encouraged that the correspondence is received through emails.***

(vii) ***Electronic files containing ID notes can be sent directly from one office to another using the e-Office, however, both the offices sending and receiving should be using e-file***

(viii) ***In e-file, a copy of the fair copy/ office copy is automatically attached in the file once the dispatch is done through the e-file.***

(ix) ***In e-file, there is a provision for setting up reminders for the reply awaited against an issue an also for sending of reminder against it.***

9. COMMUNICATIONS TO THE ATTORNEY – GENERAL OF INDIA

References to the Attorney – General should be made only by the Ministry ofLaw and Justice.

10. COMMUNICATION TO CONSTITUTIONAL / STATUTORY AUTHORITIES

References to constitutional and statutory authorities such as Election Commission of India should normally be made in the letter form addressed to Principal Secretary / Secretary. In no case office memorandum should be sent to such authorities by the Ministries / Departments.

11. COMUNICATIONS TO THE COMPTROLLER AND AUDITOR GENERAL OF INDIA

References to the Comptroller and Auditor General of India for his views or advice can be made only by or through the Ministry of Finance. In matters of day-to-day administration, Ministries / Departments may, however, correspond direct with the Comptroller and Auditor General of India at their discretion.

12. COMMUNICATIONS TO THE UNION PUBLIC SERVICE COMMISSION

References to the Union Public Service Commission should normally be made in the form of letters addressed to the Secretary. In certain matters, e.g., requisitions for recruitment, formal references should ordinarily be preceded by personal discussion at appropriate level.

13. CORRESPONDENCE WITH UNION TERRITORY ADMINISTRATIONS

All communications of a routine nature which clearly relate to the business of a particular department, should ordinarily be addressed to the Secretary in the appropriate department. Other important communications may be addressed to the Chief Secretary or the Administrator.

14. CORRESPONDENCE WITH STATE GOVERNMENT

14.1. Communications on the subjects which clearly relate to the business of a particular department should normally be addressed to the Secretary of that department. Other communications including those of special nature or importance warranting attention at higher levels, may be addressed to the Chief Secretary. Demi-official letters can also be sent to officers of State Governments. In case of demi-official communications to the Chief Secretary of a State, this level should not be below the level of Joint Secretary.

14.2. Communications other than those of a purely routine nature, e.g., acknowledgements, should not ordinarily be addressed to State Governments, except with the prior approval and over the signature of the branch officer. Purely routine communications can, however, be signed by a section officer.

15. CORRESPONDENCE WITH THE LOK SABHA AND THE RAJYA SABHA SECRETARIATS

Communications meant for the Lok Sabha Secretariat or the Rajya Sabha Secretariat and requiring urgent or high level attention may be addressed to the Secretaries concerned and not to the Speaker or the Chairman direct.

16. CORRESPONDENCE WITH MEMBERS OF PARLIAMENT

16.1. Communications received from Members of Parliament should be attended to promptly.

16.2. Where a communication is addressed to a Minister, it should, as far as practicable, be replied to by the Minister himself. In other cases, a reply should normally be issued over the signature of an officer of the rank of Secretary only.

16.3. Where, however, a communication is addressed to the head of an attached or subordinate office, Public Sector Undertakings, Financial Institutions (including nationalized banks), Division/ Branch In-charge in a Ministry / Department / Organisation, it should be replied to by the addressee himself. In routine matters, he may send an appropriate reply on his own. In policy matters, however, the officer should have prior consultation with higher authorities before sending a reply. It should, however, be ensured that minimum level at which such replies are sent to Members of Parliament is that of Under Secretary and that also in letter form only.

16.4. Normally, information sought by a Member should be supplied unless it is of such a nature that it would have been denied to him even if asked for on the floor of the Houses of Parliament.

16.5. As far as possible, in corresponding with Members of Parliament, preprinted or cyclostyled replies should be avoided.

16.6. In case a reference from an ex-Member of Parliament is addressed to a Minister or Secretary, reply to such reference may be sent by the concerned Divisional Head after obtaining approval of the Secretary of the Ministry/ Department. In case the reference is addressed to a lower level officer, reply to such reference could be sent by the officer on his own in non-policy cases and after obtaining approval of the higher authorities in policy cases. However, the minimum level at which reply could be sent should be that of an Under Secretary and that too in letter form only.

17. CORRESPONDENCE WITH MINISTERS OF STATE GOVERNMENTS

The procedure laid down in the above paragraph may also be followed in dealing with communications received from the Ministers of State Governments.

18. CORRESPONDENCE WITH FOREIGN GOVERNMENTS ANDINTERNATIONAL ORGANISATIONS

Correspondence with Foreign Governments and their Missions in India, Heads of Indian Diplomatic Missions and posts abroad and, United Nations and its specialized agencies should normally be channelized through the Ministry of External Affairs. The exceptions under which direct correspondence may be resorted to are indicated in the instructions issued by the Ministry of External Affairs.

19. PROMPT RESPONSE TO LETTERS RECEIVED

19.1. Each communication received from the Members of Parliament, a member of the public, a recognized association or a public body should be acknowledged within 15 days, followed by a reply within the next 15 days of acknowledgement sent.

19.2. Where (i) delay is anticipated in sending a final reply, or (ii) information has to be obtained from another Ministry or another office, an interim reply should be sent within a month (from the date of receipt) indicating the possible date by which a final reply can be given.

19.3. If any such communication is wrongly addressed to a department, it should be transferred promptly (within a week) to the appropriate department under intimation to the party concerned.

19.4. Where the request of a member of the public cannot be acceded to for any reason, reasons for not acceding to such a request should be given.

19.5. As far as possible, requests from members of public should be looked at from the user's point of view and not solely from the point of view of what may be administratively convenient.

20. TARGET DATE FOR REPLIES

In all important matters in which State Governments, departments of the Central Government, or other offices, public bodies or individuals are consulted, time limit for replies may ordinarily be specified. On the expiry of the specified date, orders of the appropriate authority may be obtained on whether the offices whose replies have not been received, may be allowed an extension of time or whether the matter may be processed, without waiting for their replies.

21. RESPONSIBILITY MAPPING REGARDING ISSUE OF COMMUNICATIONS

Generally the responsibility for issue of communications is as given below:

S. No.	Action	Primary Responsibility	Secondary Responsibility
1.	Fair copying the draft approved by the competent authority. This includes ensuring that all corrections made have been carried out.	Dealing Hand	Section Officer
2.	Fair copying the draft demi-official letter approved by the competent authority. This includes ensuring that all corrections made have been carried out.	Personal Staff of the officer signing the D.O. letter	Dealing Hand

S. No.	Action	Primary Responsibility	Secondary Responsibility
3.	Ensure that all enclosures are attached to the draft.	Dealing Hand	Section Officer
4.	Issue of the communications (fax or email) with enclosures, if any, as approved by the competent authority.	Personal Staff of the officer signing the D.O. letter	Dealing Hand
5.	Issue of fair Demi-Official letter with enclosures if complete set of enclosures is attached to the draft. In case, the enclosure is to be attached, the D.O. letter will be issued by the Section. This includes sending of fax or email as approved by the competent authority.	Personal Staff of the officer signing the D.O. letter	Dealing Hand
6.	In case the communication is to be issue through the Central Issue Section, making entries in the Peon/Messenger book, obtaining signature of the Central Issue Section and receiving the Peon book back for safe custody	Dealing Hand or Personal Staff of the officer signing the D.O. letter	Nil
7.	Retaining office copy of the communication sent. This includes print of emails sent, including attachment(s) or downloading and filing it in appropriate folders in e-Office system.	Dealing Hand or Personal Staff of the officer signing the D.O. letter	Section Officer or the officer concerned, if email sent by the officer

S. No.	Action	Primary Responsibility	Secondary Responsibility
8.	Docketing and referencing of office copy and safe custody of the file	Dealing Hand	Section Officer

22. CONCLUSION

Drafting is a crucial activity in officer. A good draft will result in a good communication being sent out of the office, and thus project a good image. A poor draft may not convey intentions correctly and there is always a chance to mess things up. It is therefore necessary that drafting is done skillfully and decisions are conveyed through good communications drafted in an appropriate form.

EXERCISES

EXERCISE – 1

Read the following statements and put a tick mark (✓) under the option 'True' or 'False', which you consider to be correct:

	Statement	True	False
1.	Drafting is the process of preparing a rough copy which will convey decisions/ views of the competent authority.		
2.	In e-file system, there is no provision for creating a draft.		
3.	In e-file system, once the draft is approved, no change can be made in the draft content by any authority.		
4.	In e-file, the dispatch is made electronically as well as manually and all the data relating to the issue is saved in the computer.		
5.	Electronic files containing ID notes cannot be sent directly from one office to another using the e-office even though they are using e-file system.		

EXERCISE-2

Fill in the blank in each of the following sentences by picking up the option, which you consider to be correct, from among those given below each sentence.

1. Drafting is required________________

   (a) in all cases irrespective of the fact that the case is of routine nature or of policy nature.

   (b) in cases where the line of action is not clear or where a policy decision is intended to be conveyed.

   (c) primarily because the intention is to involve a number of persons and share responsibility for conveying a decision.

   (d) to give an opportunity to officers at various levels to impress their bosses with their knowledge and skill in the use of language.

2. When a communication is of some length or complexity____________

(a) it should generally conclude with a summary.

(b) it should repeat the ideas several times so that there is no difficulty in understanding them.

(c) it should be left to the party to come to a conclusion which it thinks to be appropriate.

(d) it should so confuse the recipient that he feels compelled to do what the communication asks him to do.

3. When writing a d.o. letter, attempt should be to____________

(a) make it as lengthy as possible so that the message could be properly conveyed.

(b) give detailed arguments in the letter instead of in appendices so that reading it not interrupted.

(c) condense the message in one page in a few small paragraphs.

(d) maintain objectivity by writing it in a formal and impersonal style.

4. When it is intended that the matter raised in a communication should receive the personal attention of a particular officer, _____________.

(a) it may be addressed or marked to the officer by name.

(b) it should be sent through a formal letter addressed to the superior officer under whom that particular officer functions.

(c) it may be sent through a demi-official letter addressed to the administrative head of the organisation in which that particular officer functions.

(d) it should be sent only through a formal letter, and that particular officer may be advised to get it from the Central Registry of his Ministry or department.

5. In all important matters in which State Governments, departments of the Central Government or other offices etc. are consulted_____________.

(a) replies from these organisations should be awaited patiently and further action taken only after all replies have been received.

(b) time limits for replies may ordinarily be specified and orders of the appropriate authority obtained on the expiry of the specified date about further action to be taken.

(c) efforts should be made to contact such organisations personally and obtain their views.

(d) those organisations which fail to send their replies within a reasonable time should be reminded through strongly worded demi-official letter.

EXERCISE-3

Fill in the blank in each of the following sentences by picking up the option, which you consider to be correct, from among there given below each sentence.

1. All drafts put up on a file should bear ________________

   (a) the serial number in the dispatch register.

   (b) the serial number in the Assistant's diary at which the communication to which it is a reply was entered.

   (c) the file number.

   (d) the diary number of the section diary at which the receipt to which it is a reply was entered.

2. In writing or typing a draft__________________

   (a) sufficient space should be left on the margin and between successive lines so that additions of words may be made, if necessary.

   (b) no space should be left blank so that it becomes impossible to make any additions and alterations in the draft.

   (c) it is not necessary to give the name and designation of the officer over whose signature the communication is to issue.

   (d) it is advisable to mark "Immediate" on all drafts so that the communication is promptly attended to.

3. According to the colour code in demi-official letters, ___________.

   (a) a demi-official letter from a Minister will exhibit the National Emblem in red colour.

   (b) a demi-official letter from an official will exhibit the National Emblem in blue colour.

   (c) demi-official letter from either a Minister or an official will exhibit the National Emblem in the same green colour.

   (d) a demi-official letter from a Minister will exhibit the National Emblem in blue colour and that from an officer will exhibit the National Emblem in red colour.

4. When two or more drafts are put up on a file, ____________________.

(a) all the drafts may be bunched together with a stapler and put up.

(b) the drafts as well as the slips attached thereto should be marked 'DFAI', DFAII', and so on.

(c) one draft should be got approved first, and thereafter the next draft put up.

(d) all the drafts should be taken personally to the appropriate officer and got approved.

5. If it is necessary to refer to more than one communication or a series of communications in a draft, it should be done____________________.

(a) immediately after the salutation, and only after the reference to the communications has been completed the text of the draft reply should follow.

(b) by referring to the communications at the end immediately before superscription.

(c) by referring to the communications immediately after the first paragraph in the draft.

(d) by referring to the communications in the margin of the draft.

EXERCISE–4

1. Rural Infrastructure Development Corporation, Department of Rural Up liftment, are experiencing difficulties in carrying out their projects due to shortage of qualified Assistant Engineers (Civil). The Corporation has, therefore, proposed to the Department of Rural Up liftment to permit them to recruit on *ad hoc* basis, Assistant Engineers (Civil) by direct recruitment from the open market. But there is a Government ban on direct recruitment on *ad hoc* basis. The Department have, therefore, proposed to the Corporation to give additional charge of the vacant posts to existing incumbents and pay them remuneration according to rules.

2. Please prepare a draft reply to the Corporation on File No. **<u>A-37012/36-2021-Admn.I</u>**

EXERCISE - 5

1. Chief Engineer, Systems, Power Development Corporation, Ministry of Power Development, had deputed several officers during the last few years on U.N. assignments. On return, these officers were required to deposit the pension and other pensionary benefits received from the U.N. in the Government account and draw them when they retired from Government service.

2. With the replacement of the Foreign Exchange Regulation Act, 1973, with the Foreign Exchange Management Act, 1999, the position has changed and now a person resident in India may open, hold, and maintain with an authorized dealer in India resident foreign currency (RFC) account out of the foreign exchange received as pensionary benefits from his employer outside. The Chief Engineer Systems, has, therefore, proposed that there should now be no objection to his officers to open such an account and deposit pensionary benefits from the U.N. in this account. He has also proposed that the Corporation take up the matter with the Government.

3. Please prepare a draft letter from the Corporation to the Government in this matter.

EXERCISE – 6

1. It has been decided to transfer the following officers with immediate effect:

   1. Shri Ram Swarup Khanna, Section Officer, from Plantation I Sec. to Oil Seeds Section.
   2. Shri Mithilesh Kumar, Section Officer, from Oil Seeds Section, to Plantation I Section.
   3. Shri Kunj Behari, Section Officer, from Administration II Section to Accounts I Section.
   4. Shri Mam Chand, Section Officer, from Accounts I Section, to Administration II Section.

2. Please prepare a draft office order announcing these changes.

EXERCISE – 7

Shri Bimal Prakash, a Deputy Director in the Directorate of Health Services, under the Department of Health Affairs, has been selected by the UPSC for appointment as a

Joint Director in the Central Children Welfare Board, on deputation basis. The appointment will be with effect from 01.08.2022 for a period of five years, but initially he will be appointed for one year, extendable on year to year basis with mutual consent.

2. Please prepare a draft notification about this appointment.

EXERCISE – 8

In response to public demand and considering the need to provide housing to slum-dwellers as early as possible, the Government have decided to build one lakh dwelling units in Delhi / New Delhi, during the next two years. These dwelling units will be multi-storeyed and constructed through public-private partnership on the land occupied by slum-dwellers. The Government plan to construct dwelling units for 16 million slum population and rehabilitate them in multi-storeyed tenements away from the land occupied by them, and take up the rehabilitation work on a self-sustaining basis. Steps will also be taken to ensure that the potential for misuse of the benefits and alienation of the genuine people are reduced.

2. Please draft a Press Note announcing this decision.

EXERCISE–9

Shri Milkhi Ram, a peon in the Ministry of Power Development, had gone to his native place by taking two months, earned leave. There, he was embroiled in violent clashes with persons who were trying to grab his property. As a result, he was detained in police custody for more than 72 hours on 25.01.2022 and a case in respect of a criminal offence is being investigated by the police.

2. When this information, reached the Ministry, it was decided to issue an order suspending him from service.

3. Please draft an order suspending Shri Milkhi Ram from service.

EXERCISE – 10

Some sections of the Government employees observed a one-day strike on 25th August 2021 to protest against some policies of the Government. The Governments policy in such matters is laid down in F.R. 17(1) and the principle of 'no work, no pay', is followed in such cases.

2. Please prepare a draft D.O. letter from Joint Secretary, Department of Personnel & Training, to Joint Secretary Department of Labour Welfare, drawing attention to the Government policy and advising him to strictly enforce this policy in his Department.

EXERCISE– 11

It has been decided to amend the Central Civil Services (Conduct) Rules, 1964 to provide that a Government servant shall perform his duties in his best judgement, except when he is acting under directions of his official superior. Even in the latter case, the official superior should give his directions ordinarily in writing, and, where oral directions become unavoidable, he should confirm the same immediately thereafter. It shall also be necessary for the official superior to confirm his oral directions when a junior officer seeks such a confirmation.

2. Please draft a notification to give effect to this amendment.

EXERCISE– 12

With a view to improving the conditions of persons with disabilities and providing them an opportunity to have a dignified living through suitable jobs in the private sector, the Government have decided to appoint a high-level Commission. The Chairman of the Commission will be Shri Y.S. Sadagoplan, former Minister of Labour in the Union Cabinet, and Director, National Institute of Mentally Handicapped, Secunderabad; Director, National Institute of Orthopaedically Handicapped, Kolkatta; Director, National Institute of Visually Handicapped, Dehradun; Director, Institute of Physically Handicapped, New Delhi and a representative each from FICCI and CII, will be Members. Deputy Director, National Institute of Mentally Handicapped, Secunderabad, will be Member-Secretary. The Commission will submit its report in six months.

2. Please draft a Resolution announcing this decision.

EXERCISE– 13

The Department of Cultural Affairs wants to endorse copies of O.M. No. 25/32/2020-Estt.(D) dated 27.12.2020 and O.M. No. 28/14/2021-Estt.(D) dated 29.03.2021, to the Archaeological Survey of India for information and necessary action.

2. Please prepare a draft endorsement for the purpose.

ANSWERS

EXERCISE - 1

1. True	2. False	3. True	4. True	5. False

EXERCISE - 2

1. (b)	2. (a)	3. (c)	4. (a)	5. (b)

EXERCISE - 3

1. (c)	2. (a)	3. (d)	4. (b)	5. (d)

....

EXERCISE - 4

F. No. A-37012/36/2021-Admn. I

Government of India

DEPARTMENT OF RURAL UPLIFTMENT

New Delhi, the 12th April 2022

The Secretary

Rural Infrastructure Development Corporation

New Delhi.

Subject: Restrictions on making *ad hoc* appointment through direct recruitment.

Sir,

Please refer to your letter No. A-37012/36/2021dated 29.12.2021 on the subject cited above.

2. According to the existing instructions, persons appointed on *ad hoc* basis are to be replaced by persons appointed on a regular basis according to the Recruitment Rules of the post concerned. Whenever an appointment is made on *ad hoc* basis, the fact that such an appointment shall not bestow on the person a claim for regular appointment and that service rendered on *ad hoc* basis would not count for seniority in the post is clearly spelt out in the orders of *ad hoc* appointment.

3. Government's instructions also provide that *ad hoc* appointments should be made only in rare cases, where a post cannot be kept vacant until a regular candidate becomes available. In particular, *ad hoc* appointment by director recruitment from the open market should be avoided.

4. In view of these instructions, it is regretted that it would not be possible to agree to fill the posts of Assistant Engineers (Civil) in your Corporation on *ad hoc* appointment by direct recruitment from the open market. If the Corporation considers that the posts cannot be kept vacant for functional considerations, efforts may be made to entrust additional

charge of these posts to serving officers and pay them additional remuneration under the rules. If this is not possible, appointments by *ad hoc* promotion or *ad hoc* deputation may be considered.

Yours faithfully,

(K.R. Sankaranaryanan)

Under Secretary to the Government of India

Tel. No. 23384951

EXERCISE- 5

No. 11/31/2022-Admn. - I

Government of India

POWER DEVELOPMENT CORPORATION

(Ministry of Power Development)

New Delhi, the 17th April 2022

Secretary to the Government of India,

Ministry of Power Development,

New Delhi.

Subject: **Deputation of Central Government employees to UN organizations – Participation in UN Pension Fund Scheme.**

Sir,

According to existing instructions, when a Central Government servant, on the expiry of foreign service with U.N. Organizations, rejoins his parent office under the Government, the retirement benefits sanctioned by the U.N. are credited to the revenues of the Government, and paid to the Government servant when he finally retires from the service of the Government.

2. It has been pointed out that with the replacement of the Foreign Exchange Regulation Act, 1973, by the Foreign Exchange Management Act, 1999, a person resident in India may open, hold, and maintain with an authorized dealer in India a Resident Foreign Currency (RFC) Account out of the foreign exchange received as pensionary benefits from his employer outside. Accordingly, there should now be no objection to allow a Government servant, on return from his service with U.N. Organizations, to open a RCF account with an authorized dealer in India, and deposit the pensionary benefits received from the U.N. in this account.

3. It is requested that the Government may kindly consider this matter, and convey their decision to this Corporation at an early date.

Yours faithfully,

(Rajiv Mohan)

Secretary,

Tel. No. 23384185

No. 11/31/2022-Admn. I   Dated: the 17th April, 2022

Copy forwarded to the Chief Engineer, Systems, Power Development Corporation, New Delhi, for information with reference to their letter No. 12/3/2022-Estt. dated the 27th March 2022.

(Rajiv Mohan)

Secretary,

Tel. No. 23384185

EXERCISE – 6

No. 31/6/2022-Admin. I

Government of India

DEPARTMENT OF AGRICULTURAL AFFAIRS

New Delhi, the 11th January 2022

OFFICE ORDER

The following transfers of Section Officers are made with immediate effect:

Name of Officer	Transfer	
	From	**To**
1. Shri Ram Swarup Khanna	Plantation I Sec.	Oil Seeds Sec.
2. Shri Mithilesh Kumar	Oilseed Sec.	Plantation I Sec.
3. Shri KunjBehari	Administration II Sec.	Accounts I Sec.
4. Shri Mam Chand	Accounts I Sec.	Administration II Sec.

(Ravi Prakash)

Under Secretary to the

Government of India

Tel. No. 23383041

Copy to:

1. Shri Ram Swarup Khanna, Section Officer
2. Shri Mithilesh Kumar, Section Officer
3. Shri Kunj Behari, Section Officer
4. Shri Mam Chand, Section Officer
5. Cash Branch
6. Office order File

EXERCISE – 7

[To be published in the Gazette of India, Part I, Section 2)

Government of India

MINISTRY OF SOCIAL WELFARE

New Delhi, the 31st July 2022

NOTIFICATION

No. 18/12/2022-Admn I. The President is pleased to appoint Shri Bimal Prakash, a Deputy Director in the Directorate of Health Services under the Department of Health, as Joint Director in the Central Children Welfare Board on transfer on deputation with effect of 1st August, 2022, until further orders.

(Kirti Saran)

Deputy Secretary to the

Government of India

To

The Manager,

Government of India Press,

Faridabad.

No. 18/12/2022-Admn. I — New Delhi, the 31st July 2022

Copy forwarded for information to :

1. Director, Central Children Welfare Board, New Delhi.
2. Shri Bimal Prakash, Joint Director, Central Children Welfare Board, New Delhi.

3. Pay and Accounts Officer, Ministry of Social Welfare, New Delhi.

4. Department of Health, Nirman Bhawan, New Delhi.

5. Director of Health Services, Nirman Bhawan, New Delhi.

Sd/-

(Budh Prasad)

Under Secretary to the

Government of India

EXERCISE – 8

Not to be published or broadcast before 8.00 p.m. on Tuesday, the 25th April 2022.

PRESS NOTE

1. In response to the public demand, the Government of India have decided that one lakh dwelling units of an average of 250-300 square feet size, will be constructed for slum dwellers in the Capital over the next two years. These dwelling units will be multi-storeyed and will be constructed through public-private partnership on the land occupied by slum dwellers.

2. The Government have to plan for dwelling units for 16 million slum population. The construction of one lakh dwelling units in the next two years is a step in this direction.

3. In view of the scarce availability of land, the Government also plans rehabilitation of slum dwellers in multi-storeyed tenements away from the land occupied by them, and to take up the rehabilitation work on self-sustaining basis. The Government will also take steps to ensure that the allotment of the tenements is made in such a manner that will reduce potential for misuse and alienation, so that the benefits accrue to genuine people.

Ministry of Urban Affairs

(Slum Development Wing)

No. 39/21/2022 – SD New Delhi, the 25th April 2022

Forwarded to the Principal Information Officer, Press Information Bureau, Government of India, New Delhi, for issuing the Press Note and giving it wide publicity.

(Abhishek Singh)

Joint Secretary to the Government of India

Tel. No. 23363030

EXERCISE-9

No. 13/2/2022 – Vig.

Government of India

MINISTRY OF POWER DEVELOPMENT

New Delhi, the 1ST February 2022

ORDER

WHEREAS a case against Shri Milkhi Ram, peon, in respect of a criminal offence is under investigation.

AND WHEREAS the said Shri Milkhi Ram was detained in custody on 25th January 2022 for a period exceeding forty – eight hours.

NOW, THEREFORE, the said Shri Milkhi Ram is deemed to have been suspended with effect from the date of detention, i.e. the 25th January 2022, in terms of sub-rule 2 of Rule 10 of the Central Civil Services (Classification, Control and Appeal) Rules, 1965, and shall remain under suspension until further orders.

(R.N. Sikri)

Deputy Secretary to the

Government of India

Tel.: 23382526

Copy to :

Shri Milkhi Ram, Peon (under suspension).

Copy also forwarded to:

1. Admn. I Section
2. Accounts Section

EXERCISE –10

MADHUKAR DWIVEDI
Joint Secretary
Tel. No. 23013339

D.O. No. 33/11/2021-Estt.(B)
Government of India
DEPARTMENT OF PERSONNEL & TRAINING

New Delhi, the 12th September 2021

Dear Shri Sharma,

The policy of the Government laid down in F.R. 17(1) is that no Government servant is entitled to any pay and allowances for any period of unauthorized absence from duty. The Government have also emphasized from time to time that the principle of 'no work, no pay' should be followed in dealing with periods of unauthorized absence, including absence during strikes.

2. It has, however, come to our notice that some sections of employees from the Central Government had observed a one-day strike on 25th August 2021 to protest against some policies of the Government. All these employees who struck work on that day are to be dealt with according to the principle of "no work, no pay". Kindly ensure that this principle is strictly followed in your Department.

With regards,

Yours sincerely,

(MadhukarDwivedi)

Shri P.S. Sharma
Joint Secretary
Department of Labour Welfare
New Delhi.

EXERCISE – 11

[To be published in the Gazette of India, Part II, Section 3, Sub-section (ii)]

Government of India

Department of Personnel & Training

New Delhi, the 20th August 2021

NOTIFICATION

S.O.__________. In exercise of the powers conferred by proviso to Article 309 of the Constitution of India, the President is pleased to make the following amendments to the Central Civil Services (Conduct) Rules, 1964, namely:

In rule 3 of the Rules, the following may be substituted for the existing entry below clause 2 (i):

"(ii) No government servant shall, in the performance of his duties, or in the exercise of powers conferred on him, act otherwise than in his best judgement except when he is acting under the direction of his official superior.

"(iii) the direction of the official superior shall ordinarily be in writing. Oral direction to subordinates shall be avoided, as for as possible. Where the issue of oral direction becomes unavoidable, the official superior shall confirm it in writing immediately thereafter.

"(iv) A Government servant who has received oral direction from his official superior shall seek confirmation of the same in writing as early as possible, whereupon it shall be the duty of the official superior to confirm the direction in writing"
[No. 13/12/2021-Estts (A)]

[Vidya Bhushan]
Joint Secretary to the Government of India

To
the Manager
Government of India Press
New Delhi

EXERCISE – 12

(To be published in the Gazette of India, Part I, Section I)

No. 22/17/2021 – DDII
Government of India
Ministry of Social Welfare

New Delhi the 30th January 2021

RESOLUTION

The Government of India have had under consideration for some time the question of improving the conditions of persons with disabilities and provide them an opportunity to have a dignified living through suitable jobs in the Private Sector. As a first step in this direction, the Government have decided to set up a Commission to identify suitable jobs in the Private Sector for such persons.

2. The Commission will have the following:

(1)	Shri Y.S. Sadagopalan former Minister of Labour	Chairman
(2)	Director, National Institute of Mentally Handicapped, Secunderabad	Member
(3)	Director, National Institute of Orthopedically Handicapped, Kolkata	Member
(4)	Director, National Institute of Visually Handicapped Dehradun	Member
(5)	Director, Institute of Physically Handicapped, New Delhi	Member
(6)	A representative of the FICCI, New Delhi.	Member
(7)	A representative of the CII, New Delhi.	Member
(8)	Deputy Director, National Institute of Mentally Handicapped,Secunderabad Member Secretary	

3. The terms of reference of the Commission shall be:

1. to identify the types of industries and activities in which the persons with disabilities can be employed without compromising the quality of work;
2. to identify jobs in these industrial undertakings or production units which the persons with disabilities may perform;
3. to suggest measures for ensuring employment of persons with disabilities in identified jobs;
4. to suggest any other measures which the Commission may consider appropriate for improving the employability of persons with disabilities.

4. The Commission may invite such other experts in the area of employment of persons with disabilities as may be considered necessary to participate in the deliberations of the Commission.

5. The Commission may devise its own procedure to carry out its work.

6. The expenditure on the pay and allowances, including T.A./D.A. etc., shall be borne from the budget of the Ministry of Social Welfare.

7. The Commission shall submit its reports within six months from the date of issue of this Resolution.

(R.K. Madhusudan)
Joint Secretary to the Government of India

ORDER

ORDERED that a copy of the Resolution be communicated to the Chairman, and Members of the Commission.

ORDERED also that the Resolution be published in the Gazette of India for general information.

(R.K. Madhusudan)
Joint Secretary to the Government of India

To

The Manager,
Government of India Press,
Faridabad.

EXERCISE – 13

NO. 12/35/2021-COORD.
GOVERNMENT OF INDIA
DEPARTMENT OF CULTURAL AFFAIRS

New Delhi, the 20th January 2021

A copy each of the under-mentioned papers is forwarded to the Archaeological Survey of India for information and necessary action.

(Ram Prasad)
Under Secretary to the Govt. of India
Tel. No. 23385457

List of papers forwarded:

1. O.M. No. 25/32/2020-Estt. (D) dated 27.12.2020
2. O.M. No. 28/14/2021-Estt. (D) dated 29.3.2021